Course 1

Steck-Vaughn

REV it up!

Robust Encounters with Vocabulary

Isabel L. Beck, Ph.D., and
Margaret G. McKeown, Ph.D.

Steck
Vaughn™

www.Steck-Vaughn.com
1-800-531-5015

D1067115

Acknowledgments

Literature

Grateful acknowledgment is given to the following publishers and copyrights owners for permissions granted to reprint selections from their publications. All possible care has been taken to trace ownership and secure permission for each selection included. In the case of any errors or omissions, the Publisher will be pleased to make suitable acknowledgments in future editions.

p. 9, "Stowaway" by Armando Soccarras Ramírez. Reprinted with permission from the January 1970 Reader's Digest. Copyright © 1970 by The Reader's Digest Assn., Inc.

p. 22, "The Princess and the Tin Box" (1948) from *The Beast in Me and Other Animals* by James Thurber. Reprinted by permission of The Barbara Hogenson Agency, Inc.

p. 33, "Did Animals Sense Tsunami Was Coming?" by Maryann Mott from *National Geographic News*, January 4, 2005. Reprinted by permission of The National Geographic Society.

p. 45, From RIVER THUNDER by Will Hobbs, copyright © 1997 by Will Hobbs. Used by permission of Dell Publishing, a division of Random House, Inc.

p. 56, "Getups" from WOULDN'T TAKE NOTHING FOR MY JOURNEY NOW by Maya Angelou, copyright © 1993 by Maya Angelou. Used by permission of Random House, Inc.

p. 68, "Bethany Hamilton: A Surfer Worth Watching," reprinted by permission of Roy Hofstetter, Business and Media Manager for Bethany Hamilton.

p. 70, "How to Play Baseball with One Hand" by Jim Abbott, reprinted by permission of the author. To learn more about Jim Abbott, go to www.jimabbott.info.

p. 81, "He—y, Come on Ou—t!" by Shinichi Hoshi, translated by Stanleigh Jones, from *The Best Japanese Science-Fiction Stories*, edited by John L. Apostolou and Martin H. Greenberg. Copyright © 1978 by Shinichi Hoshi, reprinted by permission of Barricade Books.

p. 94, "Identity" by Julio Noboa Polanco, reprinted by permission of the author.

p. 116, Excerpt from *Life of Pi*, (Canongate Books Ltd., 2002/Alfred A. Knopf Canada, 2001) © 2001 by Yann Martel. With permission of the author.

p. 116, Excerpt from LIFE OF PI, copyright © 2001 by Yann Martel, reprinted by permission of Harcourt, Inc.

p. 128, "The Living Kuan-yin" from SWEET AND SOUR: Tales From China. Copyright © 1978 by Carol Kendall and Yao-wen Li. Reprinted by permission of Clarion Books, an imprint of Houghton Mifflin Company. All rights reserved.

p. 128, From *Sweet and Sour: Tales from China* by Carol Kendall and Yao-wen Li, published by The Bodley Head. Reprinted by permission of The Random House Group Ltd.

p. 141, From MIRACLE IN THE ANDES by Nando Parrado and Vince Rause, copyright © 2006 by Nando Parrado. Used by permission of Crown Publishers, a division of Random House, Inc.

p. 154, From THE STORY OF MY LIFE by Helen Keller, edited by Roger Shattuck. Copyright © 2003 by Roger Shattuck. Used by permission of W. W. Norton & Company, Inc.

p. 166, "Animal Liberation" by Genny Lim. Reprinted by permission of the author.

p. 178, Excerpt from "The First Emperor" in *The Tomb Robbers*. Copyright © 1980 by Daniel Cohen. Reprinted by permission of the Author and his Agents, Henry Morrison, Inc.

p. 191, "How to Be Madder than Captain Ahab" by Ray Bradbury. Reprinted by permission of Don Congdon Associates, Inc. Copyright © 1973 by Scholastic Magazines, renewed 2001 by Ray Bradbury.

Cover photo ©Jeff Flindt/NewSport/Corbis.

Acknowledgments for photography and illustrations can be found on page 208.

Contents

Stowaway

By Armando Socarras Ramírez
(as told to Denis Fodor and John Reddy)

Seventeen-year-old Armando Socarras Ramírez, along with his friend Jorge Pérez Blanco decide to leave their home country of Cuba in search of freedom. But before they can begin their new life in Spain, they have to survive the journey.

The jet engines of the Iberia Airlines DC-8 thundered in earsplitting crescendo as the big plane taxied toward where we huddled in the tall grass just off the end of the runway at Havana's[1] José Martí Airport. For months, my friend Jorge Pérez Blanco and I had been planning to stow away in a wheel well on this flight, No. 904— Iberia's once-weekly, nonstop run from Havana to Madrid.[2] Now, in the late afternoon of June 3, 1970, our moment had come.

We realized that we were pretty young to be taking such a big gamble; I was seventeen, Jorge sixteen. But we were both determined to escape from Cuba, and our plans had been carefully made. We knew that departing airliners taxied[3] to the end of the 11,500-foot runway, stopped momentarily after turning around, then roared at full throttle[4] down the runway to take off. We wore rubber-soled shoes to aid us in crawling up the wheels and carried ropes to secure ourselves inside the wheel well.[5] We had also stuffed cotton in our ears as protection against the shriek of the four jet engines. Now we lay sweating with fear as the massive craft swung into its about-face, the jet blast flattening the grass all around us. "Let's run!" I shouted to Jorge.

We dashed onto the runway and sprinted toward the left-hand wheels of the momentarily stationary plane. As Jorge began to scramble up the 42-inch-high tires, I saw there was not room for us both in the single well. "I'll try the other side!" I shouted. Quickly I climbed onto the right wheels, grabbed a strut,[6] and, twisting and wriggling, pulled myself into the semi-dark well. The plane began rolling immediately, and I grabbed some machinery to keep from falling out. The roar of the engines nearly deafened me.

As we became airborne, the huge double wheels, scorching hot from takeoff, began folding into the compartment. I tried to flatten myself against the overhead as they came closer and closer; then, in desperation, I pushed at them with my feet. But they pressed powerfully upward, squeezing me terrifyingly against the roof of the well. Just when I felt that I would be crushed, the wheels locked in place and the bay doors beneath them closed, plunging me into darkness. So there I was, my five-foot-four-inch, 140-pound frame literally wedged in amid a spaghetti-like maze of conduits[7] and machinery. I could not move enough to tie myself to anything, so I stuck my rope behind a pipe.

FOOTNOTES
1. *Havana:* the capital city of Cuba
2. *Madrid:* the capital city of Spain
3. *taxied:* drove slowly
4. *full throttle:* with as much energy as possible
5. *wheel well:* the space in an airplane where the plane's wheels are stored during flight
6. *strut:* a board or pole used to support something
7. *conduits:* tubes or pipes

Then, before I had time to catch my breath, the bay doors suddenly dropped open again and the wheels stretched out into their landing position. I held on for dear life, swinging over the abyss, wondering if I had been spotted, if even now the plane was turning back to hand me over to Castro's[8] police.

By the time the wheels began retracting again, I had seen a bit of extra space among all the machinery where I could safely squeeze. Now I knew there *was* room for me, even though I could scarcely breathe. After a few minutes, I touched one of the tires and found that it had cooled off. I swallowed some aspirin tablets against the head-splitting noise[9] and began to wish that I had worn something warmer than my light sport shirt and green fatigues[10] . . . .

Shivering uncontrollably from the bitter cold, I wondered if Jorge had made it into the other wheel well and began thinking about what had brought me to this desperate situation. . . .

Young as I was, I was tired of living in a state that controlled *everyone's* life. . . . I thought more and more of trying to get away. But how? . . .

My hopes seemed futile. Then I met Jorge. . . . I found out that Jorge, like myself, was disillusioned with Cuba. "The system takes away your freedom—forever," he complained.

Jorge told me about the weekly flight to Madrid. Twice we went to the airport to reconnoiter.[11] Once a DC-8 took off and flew directly over us; the wheels were still down, and we could see into the well compartments. "There's enough room in there for me," I remember saying.

These were my thoughts as I lay in the freezing darkness more than five miles above the Atlantic Ocean. By now we had been in the air about an hour, and I was getting lightheaded from the lack of oxygen. . . . I drifted into unconsciousness.

. . . With the end of the 5,563-mile flight in sight, Captain Vara del Rey began his descent toward Madrid's Barajas Airport. Arrival would be at 8 A.M. local time, the captain told his passengers over the intercom, and the weather in Madrid was sunny and pleasant.

FOOTNOTES
. . . .
[8] *Castro:* Fidel Castro, the president of Cuba
[9] *head-splitting noise:* loud and painful noise
[10] *fatigues:* a soldier's uniform
[11] *reconnoiter:* explore and look for information

Shortly after passing over Toledo,[12] Vara del Rey let down his landing gear. As always, the maneuver was accompanied by a buffeting as the wheels hit the slipstream[13] and a 200-m.p.h. turbulence swirled through the wheel wells. Now the plane went into its final approach; now, a spurt of flame and smoke from the tires as the DC-8 touched down at about 140 m.p.h.

It was a perfect landing—no bumps. After a brief postflight check, Vara del Rey walked down the ramp steps and stood by the nose of the plane. . . .

Nearby, there was a sudden, soft plop as the frozen body of Armando Socarras fell to the concrete apron beneath the plane. José Rocha Lorenzana, a security guard, was the first to reach the crumpled figure. "When I touched his clothes, they were frozen as stiff as wood," Rocha said. "All he did was make a strange sound. . . ."

"I couldn't believe it at first," Vara del Rey said when told of Armando. "But then I went over to see him. He had ice over his nose and mouth. And his color. . ." As he watched the unconscious boy being bundled into a truck, the captain kept exclaiming to himself; "Impossible! Impossible!"

The first thing I remember after losing consciousness was hitting the ground at the Madrid airport. Then I blacked out[14] again and woke up later at the Gran Hospital de la Beneficencia[15] in downtown Madrid, more dead than alive. When they took my temperature, it was so low that it did not even register on the thermometer. "Am I in Spain?" was my first question. And then, "Where's Jorge?" (Jorge is believed to have been knocked down by the jet blast while trying to climb into the other wheel well, and to be in prison in Cuba.)

Doctors said later that my condition was comparable to that of a patient undergoing "deep-freeze" surgery—a delicate process performed only under carefully controlled conditions. Dr. José María Pajares, who cared for me, called my survival a "medical miracle," and, in truth, I feel lucky to be alive.

FOOTNOTES
[12] *Toledo:* a city in central Spain, just south of Madrid
[13] *slipstream:* a stream of air that flows behind a flying airplane
[14] *blacked out:* lost consciousness
[15] *Gran Hospital de la Beneficencia:* a large hospital in Madrid, Spain

A few days after my escape, I was up and around the hospital, playing cards with my police guard and reading stacks of letters from all over the world. I especially liked one from a girl in California. "You are a hero," she wrote, "but not very wise." My uncle, Elo Fernandez, who lives in New Jersey, telephoned and invited me to the United States to live with him. The International Rescue Committee arranged my passage and has continued to help me.

I am fine now. I live with my uncle and go to school to learn English. . . . I want to be a good citizen and contribute something to this country, for I love it here. You can smell freedom in the air. . . .

Explain Yourself

Answer each question on a separate piece of paper. Be sure to explain your answers.

1. If you wanted to bring the music on the radio to a **crescendo**, what would you do?

2. If you looked into an **abyss**, would you feel frightened? Explain.

3. Would you want to ride in a car with a **retractable** roof? Why or why not?

4. What might cause you to be **disillusioned** with your favorite celebrity?

5. In what sports do athletes **buffet** each other? Explain.

6. What might make you move **turbulently**?

7. How can you tell if people are **conspiring**?

8. If you thought your friend was behaving **imprudently**, what would you say to him or her?

9. What could you do to prove to your friends that you are **intrepid**?

10. If you were arranging a **clandestine** meeting, where would you have it? Why?

VOCABULARY

crescendo A crescendo is a sound that gets louder and louder.

abyss An abyss is a hole or space so big and deep that it seems bottomless.

retract If something retracts, it pulls back or in.

disillusioned If you are disillusioned, you realize that something or someone is not as good as you thought.

buffet If something buffets something else, it hits or pushes it violently and repeatedly.

turbulence Turbulence is a disturbance that is caused by wild, unpredictable, and constantly changing conditions.

conspire When people conspire to do something, they secretly plan to do it.

imprudent When you do something imprudent, you act without thinking through the consequences.

intrepid An intrepid person is brave and determined and doesn't let obstacles get in the way.

clandestine A clandestine act is done in secret, probably because it is wrong or illegal.

Take It Further

Complete these sentences on a separate piece of paper.

1. Outside my window, I could hear the **crescendo** of . . .

2. Jamie was scared to go near the **abyss** because . . .

3. It's a good idea to **retract** your umbrella when . . .

4. Harrison was **disillusioned** about Sophie because . . .

5. At the concert, Miranda was **buffeted** by . . .

6. The **turbulence** during our trip made me . . .

7. Logan thought that his friends were **conspiring** when he saw . . .

8. People thought that Maya was **imprudent** because she was always . . .

9. We knew the newspaper reporter was **intrepid** after she . . .

10. Marcos knew he had to keep his activities **clandestine** because . . .

Explore It

Many words are formed by combining a root word with a prefix. Attaching a prefix to the beginning of a word changes the word's meaning. For example, if you attach the prefix *im–* to the word *possible*, you can tell that *im–* means "not."

Work in a group and study the word *imprudent*. Create a skit about people who do something *imprudent*. Create two different endings for your skit, one in which the characters continue to be *imprudent* and one in which they become *prudent*. Perform both versions of the skit for the class, and have your classmates identify which ending belongs with which word.

Storm Chasers

What do you do when you hear the crescendo of a thunderstorm coming toward you? If you're like most people, you probably don't grab your video camera, jump in your car, and drive toward the storm. Then again, most people aren't storm chasers. We sat down with storm chaser Harry Kane and asked him about his thrilling hobby.

Q: What exactly is a storm chaser?

Harry Kane (H.K.): Storm chasers are people who travel to watch or chase storms. Some of us are scientists who study weather. Some are weather photographers. Storm chasers try to predict when and where big storms will happen. We want to see those storms in action.

Q: Isn't storm chasing dangerous? It seems crazy to head toward a violent storm.

H.K.: You're right! Heading into a storm imprudently can be very risky. Storm chasers face lots of obstacles, from hail and tornadoes to dangerous road conditions. We must be ready to get out of the way when lightning strikes or when wind buffets the car too strongly.

Q: What's the most exciting thing that's happened to you on a chase?

H.K.: Like lots of storm chasers, I always wanted to see a tornado. They're rare. You don't see one every time you go into a storm. During one storm, though, I saw three tornadoes—and one of them headed straight for me! I drove away as fast as I could. In my car's mirror, I could see trees being pulled out of the ground behind me. It was a scary experience, but it was also a sight I'll never forget.

15

Lea Davis STORM CHASER

The weather had been beautiful, warm, and sunny all week, but my vacation wasn't about relaxing on a beach somewhere. My aunt Lisa is a scientist who studies weather. She'd taken me on a storm-chasing trip in Oklahoma. It sounded so exciting when Aunt Lisa invited me. I even started thinking of myself as an intrepid weather explorer. Armed only with a camera, I'd brave wild winds and fiery lightning bolts. I could call myself Lea Davis, Storm Chaser! I'd be a hero!

Okay, maybe I got a little carried away, but I don't think that seeing a simple thunderstorm is too much to ask. Under clear blue Oklahoma skies, Aunt Lisa and I ate scrambled eggs in diners and sat in our motel room doing crossword puzzles. It was definitely not my idea of a thrilling vacation. Who wants to be Lea Davis, Crossword Puzzle Finisher?

By the time our trip was over, I was feeling pretty disappointed. As we pulled out of the motel driveway, I decided to take a nap and forget the trip ever happened. When Aunt Lisa woke me, the first thing I noticed was the black sky. Straight ahead of us was a huge, turbulent thunderstorm.

The storm was a couple of miles away, and Aunt Lisa said it wouldn't be safe to get any closer, so we pulled over and watched as it flashed and rumbled across the plains. We saw a couple of little funnel clouds trying to turn into tornadoes, but the funnels never touched the ground. I got some great pictures, and watching the storm was one of the most exciting things I've ever done. I wasn't exactly a hero, but I was finally a real storm chaser.

Rev Up Your Writing

What do you think about storm chasers? Would you ever want to chase storms? Explain why or why not. Use as many of the vocabulary words as possible but make sense.

Word Organizer

Copy this graphic organizer onto a separate piece of paper.

Think of words that describe the word *intrepid* and write your answers in the ovals. Then give examples of things that an intrepid person might do and write your answers in the boxes. Explain your answers.

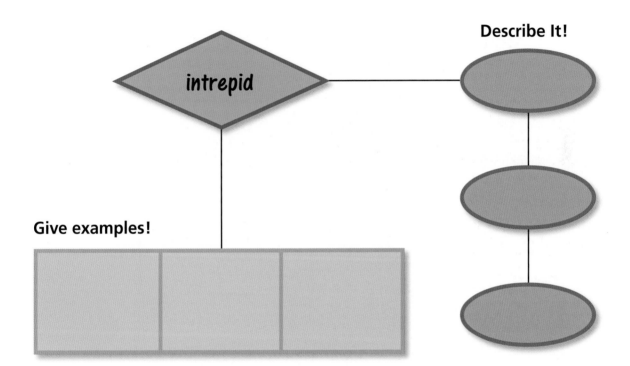

Describe It!

intrepid

Give examples!

Peter's Prank

Monday

Jorge–
Hi from camp! You won't believe what just happened. Last night, campers from the cabin next door snuck into our cabin, took our shoes, and hung them from the dining hall ceiling! It took us hours to get our shoes down. My friend Mike says we should play a prank in return, but I'm not so sure.

–Peter

Tuesday

Jorge–
Just when I thought things were calming down, we have been attacked again! Someone put worms in our sneakers. It was disgusting! You know how I've always said it's not nice to get revenge? Well, I'm retracting that statement. I'd like to drop the other cabin into an abyss. That doesn't seem very practical, though. Do you have any ideas?

–Peter

Jorge Lope
25 Vice R
Austin, TX 78

Wednesday

Jorge–
It's official——I am a genius. Okay, the people in my cabin are pretty smart, too. At long last, we've come up with the perfect prank. We had a clandestine meeting last night to work out the details, and we've conspired to collect our supplies today. I've got to run, but I'll let you know what happens.

–Peter

Jorge L
253 V
Austin

Thursday

Jorge–
We did it! Last night, after everyone was asleep, we snuck into their cabin. We wound a ball of yarn all around the cabin, tied it in knots, and covered the yarn with honey. This morning, they woke up and realized they were stuck in a tangled, sticky web! They had to untangle the whole thing. It was hilarious.

–Peter

Jorge Lope
253 Vice Road
Austin, TX 78360

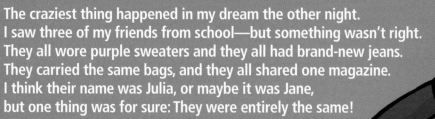

Identity CRISIS!

The craziest thing happened in my dream the other night.
I saw three of my friends from school—but something wasn't right.
They all wore purple sweaters and they all had brand-new jeans.
They carried the same bags, and they all shared one magazine.
I think their name was Julia, or maybe it was Jane,
but one thing was for sure: They were entirely the same!

I felt a rush of panic as I looked down at my clothes,
my purple sweater, brand-new jeans. Where had I
   gotten those?
I started getting worried when I realized with a start
that no one in the world could tell the four of us apart.
And if we were so similar, there was no guarantee
that I would know which girl was which, or which of them
   was me!

I woke up feeling nervous but I knew I had to call
my friends before we all turned into zombies from the mall.
"You guys," I said, "we've got to fix this problem right away.
I want to feel original when I get dressed each day.
I've gotten disillusioned with the clothes we always wear,
and I'd rather eat a worm than spend five hours on my hair."

I thought they would be mad, but to my shock, they all agreed
that we should try to separate our shared identity.
I found an old propeller hat I hadn't worn for years,
I draped myself with feathers, and I went to face my fears.
I knew that I looked goofy, but I didn't care because
at least everyone else would know exactly who I was.

Rev Up Your Writing

Both Peter and the girl in the poem had creative ideas. Write about a crazy or creative idea you or someone you know has had and describe how other people reacted to the idea. Use as many of the vocabulary words as possible but make sense.

Can You Relate?

Copy this graphic organizer onto a separate piece of paper. Match the following words with their related vocabulary word. If a word relates to both vocabulary words, explain why.

agitate   If someone is agitated, he or she is obviously upset or worried.
cacophony   A cacophony is a loud, unpredictable, and unpleasant noise.
clamor   If someone clamors, they make a lot of noise by shouting.
riotous   When something is riotous, it is wild and uncontrollable.
sonorous   A sonorous instrument makes a clear, loud sound.

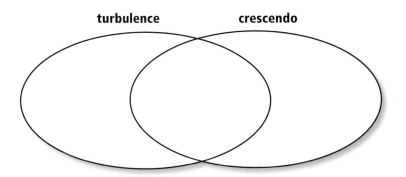

turbulence   crescendo

In Your Own Words

Respond to one of the following prompts on a separate piece of paper. As you respond, use as many of the vocabulary words as possible. Be creative but make sense!

▶ Write about a time when you or someone you know took a trip. Describe the place you visited and what the trip was like.

▶ Write a biography about someone who took a risk. What did he or she do? How did it turn out? How has the person inspired you?

▶ Write about a topic of your choice.

VOCABULARY

crescendo
abyss
retract
disillusioned
buffet
turbulence
conspire
imprudent
intrepid
clandestine

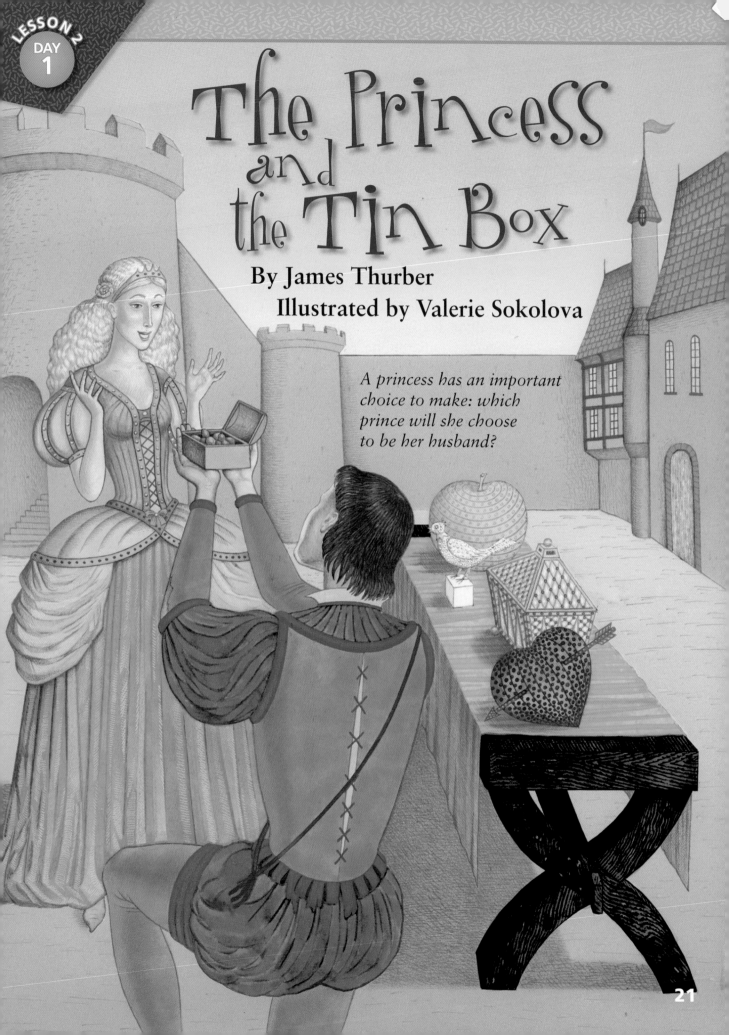

The Princess and the Tin Box

By James Thurber

Illustrated by Valerie Sokolova

A princess has an important choice to make: which prince will she choose to be her husband?

Once upon a time, in a far country, there lived a King whose daughter was the prettiest princess in the world. Her eyes were like the cornflower,[1] her hair was sweeter than the hyacinth,[2] and her throat made the swan look dusty.[3]

From the time she was a year old, the Princess had been showered with presents. Her nursery looked like Cartier's[4] window. Her toys were all made of gold or platinum or diamonds or emeralds. She was not permitted to have wooden blocks or china dolls or rubber dogs or linen books, because such materials were considered cheap for the daughter of a king.

When she was seven, she was allowed to attend the wedding of her brother and throw real pearls at the bride instead of rice. Only the nightingale, with his lyre[5] of gold, was permitted to sing for the Princess. The common blackbird, with his boxwood flute, was kept out of the palace grounds. She walked in silver-and-samite[6] slippers to a sapphire-and-topaz[7] bathroom and slept in an ivory bed inlaid with rubies.

On the day the Princess was eighteen, the King sent a royal ambassador to the courts of five neighboring kingdoms to announce that he would give his daughter's hand in marriage to the prince who brought her the gift she liked the most.

The first prince to arrive at the palace rode a swift white stallion and laid at the feet of the Princess an enormous apple made of solid gold which he had taken from a dragon who had guarded it for a thousand years. It was placed on a long ebony table set up to hold the gifts of the Princess' suitors. The second prince, who came on a gray charger, brought her a nightingale made of a thousand diamonds, and it was placed beside the golden apple. The third prince, riding on a black horse, carried a great jewel box made of platinum and sapphires, and it was placed next to the diamond nightingale. The fourth prince, astride a fiery yellow horse, gave the Princess a gigantic heart made of rubies and pierced by an emerald arrow. It was placed next to the platinum-and-sapphire jewel box.

Now the fifth prince was the strongest and handsomest of all the five suitors, but he was the son of a poor king whose realm had been overrun by mice and locusts and wizards and mining engineers so that there was nothing much of value left in it. He came plodding up to the palace of the Princess on a plow horse, and he brought her a small tin box filled with mica and feldspar and hornblende[8] which he had picked up on the way.

The other princes roared with disdainful laughter when they saw the tawdry gift the fifth prince had brought to the Princess. But she examined it with great interest and squealed with delight, for all her life she had been glutted with precious stones and priceless metals, but she had never seen tin before or mica or feldspar or hornblende. The tin box was placed next to the ruby heart pierced with an emerald arrow.

"Now," the King said to his daughter, "you must select the gift you like best and marry the prince that brought it."

The Princess smiled and walked up to the table and picked up the present she liked the most. It was the platinum-and-sapphire jewel box, the gift of the third prince.

"The way I figure it," she said, "is this. It is a very large and expensive box, and when I am married, I will meet many admirers who will give me precious gems with which to fill it to the top. Therefore, it is the most valuable of all the gifts my suitors have brought me, and I like it the best."

The Princess married the third prince that very day in the midst of great merriment and high revelry.[9] More than a hundred thousand pearls were thrown at her and she loved it.

Moral: All those who thought that the Princess was going to select the tin box filled with worthless stones instead of one of the other gifts will kindly stay after class and write one hundred times on the blackboard, "I would rather have a hunk of aluminum silicate than a diamond necklace."

Explain Yourself

Answer each question on a separate piece of paper. Be sure to explain your answers.

1. What is one **realm** that you would like to control?

2. If you see your friend **plodding** toward his bus, what would you think? Why?

3. Why might the president of the chess club be **disdainful** of the captain of the football team?

4. Would you be upset if you lost the **tawdry** necklace that an old friend gave you? Why or why not?

5. Would you sell lemonade at a carnival **glutted** with juice and soda stands? Why or why not?

6. Would you be friends with a person who **derided** you daily? Explain.

7. Would a student who takes **copious** notes earn a good grade? Why or why not?

8. How would you feel if your talent show performance was **eclipsed** by your best friend's performance? Why?

9. At what amount would you **appraise** a diamond-covered baseball bat? Explain.

10. Would it be **ironic** if your dentist had cavities? Why or why not?

VOCABULARY

realm   A realm is an area under someone or something's control.

plod   Someone who plods walks slowly and heavily, without much energy or excitement.

disdainful   If you are disdainful, you look down on others because you believe you are better.

tawdry   Something tawdry is cheap looking and usually in bad taste.

glut   If you are glutted with something, you have so much of it you can never use it all.

deride   If you deride someone or something, you laugh at it and make fun of it.

copious   If you have a copious amount of something, you have a lot of it.

eclipse   If something eclipses something else, it takes the attention away from it by being larger or more important.

appraise   When you appraise something, you decide how valuable you think it is.

ironic   If something is ironic, it is strange or funny because it is the opposite of what you would expect.

Take It Further

Complete these sentences on a separate piece of paper.

1. Because it was outside his **realm**, the king did not . . .

2. When I saw Roger **plodding** across the field after his game, I knew . . .

3. Lorna became **disdainful** of the other girls in the group after . . .

4. I would wear **tawdry** clothing to . . .

5. Tamyra's closet was **glutted** with shoes, so she . . .

6. Jeff's older brother Omar is always **deriding** him for . . .

7. My friend talks so **copiously** that . . .

8. My plans to hang out at the mall were **eclipsed** by . . .

9. Jordan's collection of comic books was **appraised** at . . .

10. It was **ironic** that Andrea won the dance competition because . . .

Explore It

The Story of *Tawdry*

Imagine getting throat cancer because you wore tawdry necklaces. Well that's the legend of Saint Audrey. Saint Audrey was once Queen of Northumbria. Supposedly, she gave up her throne to live in a religious community. As a younger woman, she loved to wear fancy laces around her neck. When she later got throat cancer, she blamed her misfortune on the fancy lace she used to wear. *Tawdry lace*, or lace worn by women around the throat, is named after her (Sain**t** + **Audrey**).

Words like *tawdry* are sometimes referred to as portmanteau (port man TOE) words. Portmanteau words combine two different words to form a new word.

Use the following word pairs to make common portmanteau words:

1. smoke/fog

2. breakfast/lunch

3. spoon/fork

4. skirt/shorts

5. alpha/beta

6. cybernetic/organism

MangAnime

If you're like many kids in America, you have probably read a comic strip or two in your lifetime. These printed cartoons that tell a story can be found on the back of cereal boxes, in your town's newspaper, and in comic books. Comics can also be found halfway around the world, in Japan. Japanese-style comics are known as *manga* (MAHN gah). Many types of *manga* exist in Japan, the United States, and other parts of the world. Very popular *manga* are often turned into *anime* (AH nee may), or a Japanese-style cartoon series (*anime* is short for *animation*).

Read the timeline to learn more about *manga* (Japanese-style comics) and *anime* (Japanese-style animation).

1100s

Pre-*Manga*: Japanese artist Toba Sojo created *Choujuugiga* (or *Scrolls of Frolicking Animals*) that show animals behaving like humans. Many of these scrolls were used to keep track of time. They can be thought of as early *manga* because the pictures sometimes told a story.

1800s

Around the year 1812, a Japanese artist known as Katsushika Hokusai created "whimsical pictures." Hokusai sketched thousands of pictures, including pictures of landscapes and animals. He also developed *Hokusai manga* using a wood-block-printed copybook.

1947

Osamu Tezuka wrote *Shintakarajima* (or *New Treasure Island*), the world's first modern *manga*. This 200-page *manga*, called a graphic novel because of its length, changed the realm of comics by adding movie techniques, including close-ups of characters. Tezuka also added bold lines and other artistic elements found in traditional western cartoons.

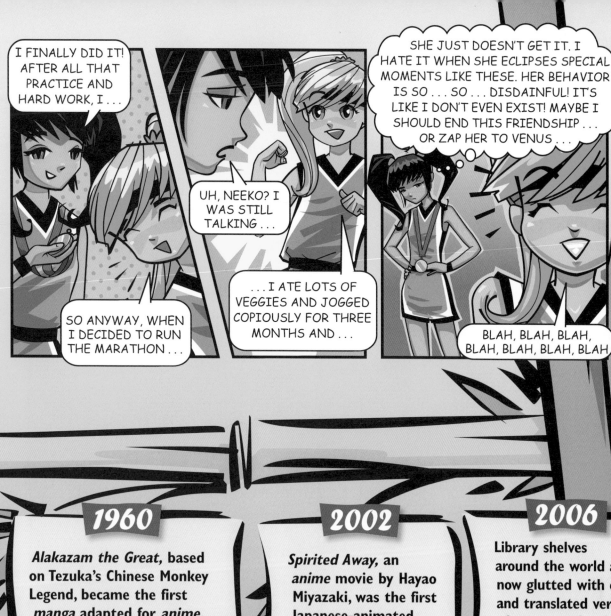

1960

Alakazam the Great, based on Tezuka's Chinese Monkey Legend, became the first *manga* adapted for *anime.*

1961

Tezuka founded one of Japan's first TV animation studios, Mushi Productions. Tezuka incorporated the use of large eyes and big heads to create a variety of emotional expressions and moods. This artistic style of animation can be seen in today's *manga* and *anime.*

2002

Spirited Away, an *anime* movie by Hayao Miyazaki, was the first Japanese-animated feature film to receive an Academy Award® for Best Animated Film in America.

2006

Library shelves around the world are now glutted with original and translated versions of *manga* and *anime.* From science fiction to comedy, from romance to fantasy, people of all ages continue to enjoy this Japanese art form.

Rev Up Your Writing

Have you ever known anyone like the character Neeko? Would you be friends with this kind of person? Explain why or why not. Use as many vocabulary words as possible but make sense.

27

Word Organizer

Copy this graphic organizer onto a separate piece of paper.

Write an explanation of the word *copious* in the Explain It box below. Then write a sentence using the word *copious* in the Use It box. Finally, use the Sketch It box to sketch a picture that shows the word *copious*. Explain your work.

copious Write It	 Explain It
    Use It	 Sketch It

Portraits of Culture

Sakura
Cherry Blossoms

Cherry Blossoms are often seen in *anime*. They are used as a symbol of a life cut tragically short because the blossoms fall when they are at their peak. In Japan, blossom-viewing parties and picnics are a tradition. They are held during the spring when the cherry trees drop their blossoms all at once. Sakura is also a very popular girl's name in Japan.

Gakkoa
School

Middle school students in Japan stay in the same classroom for most of the day. All the students are responsible for keeping the room clean. Students plod through difficult lessons together. Instead of deriding struggling classmates, advanced students help others do their work and stay on task.

READ IT RIGHT

In America, we read from left to right and top to bottom. Not so in Japan! There, people read things from top to bottom first, then from right to left. Books open from what we would consider the back. To make reading *manga* a little easier for American readers, the pictures in some of the books are switched. They are flipped horizontally to reflect a mirror image. This allows the comic strip to stay in order without making the images look weird.

29

EXPLORE the Art of Anime

Jay Alexander of Animated Writers, Inc., discusses the art of *anime* with Annie-Mae Shun, legendary *anime* artist.

Q: Annie-Mae, one of the things I've noticed about the art of *anime* is that most characters look American. This seems a little ironic.

Annie-Mae Shun (A. S.): Ah, yes. Tezuka and other founding fathers of *manga* and *anime* chose to adapt the style and bold features of popular western cartoons. American-looking characters have made it easier for writers and translators to adjust *manga* and *anime* plots and characters to fit American taste.

Q: Can you tell me about the colors? What do they mean?

A. S.: *Anime* colors, especially hair colors, can help you appraise a character's personality. A red-haired character may be a little more lively and demanding. Characters with wild styles or bizarrely colored hair may have special powers. And blondes are often stuck up and disdainful of others.

Q: Tell me about the eyes. Why are they so big?

A. S.: Well, they're not *all* big. The bigger the eyes are, the more innocent the character is. Osamu Tezuka added this feature to his characters so he could more accurately illustrate the characters' emotions.

Q: Thank you, Annie-Mae Shun, for helping us understand a little more about the art of *anime*!

A. S.: It's always a pleasure.

Don't judge a person by the clothes they wear; a tawdry appearance often conceals a priceless spirit. —Anonymous

Rev Up Your Writing

Can you think of any colors that represent something? What are they? What do they represent? Explain why you think they are a symbol for that thing. Use as many of the vocabulary words as possible but make sense.

Can You Relate?

Copy this graphic organizer onto a separate piece of paper. Match the following words with their related vocabulary word. If a word relates to more than one vocabulary word, explain why.

affront   An affront is an obvious or intentional insult.
antithetical   Something that is antithetical is the exact opposite of what was expected.
jurisdiction   The police's jurisdiction is the area in which they have power.
lampoon   A story that makes fun of people is called a lampoon.
sarcastic   People who are sarcastic say the opposite of what they really mean in order to make fun of or hurt others.

deride	realm	ironic

In Your Own Words

Respond to one of the following prompts on a separate piece of paper. As you respond, use as many of the vocabulary words as possible. Be creative but make sense!

▶ Write about a time when you or someone you know received a gift that you didn't like. What was the situation? Why didn't you like the gift? What did you do?

▶ You work for a Web site devoted to all things *manga*. You receive an e-mail from a fan wanting help creating characters for her new *manga* comic. Write an advice column giving her some ideas. Give your characters names, appearances, and personalities.

▶ Write about a topic of your choice.

VOCABULARY

realm
plod
disdainful
tawdry
glut
deride
copious
eclipse
appraise
ironic

DID ANIMALS SENSE TSUNAMI WAS COMING?

By Maryann Mott

Before the tsunami struck the coastlines of India and Sri Lanka, many animals started behaving strangely. Did these animals somehow know that the terrible tsunami was coming?

Before giant waves slammed into Sri Lanka and India coastlines ten days ago, wild and domestic animals seemed to know what was about to happen and fled to safety.

According to eyewitness accounts, the following events happened:

- Elephants screamed and ran for higher ground.
- Dogs refused to go outdoors.
- Flamingos abandoned their low-lying breeding areas.
- Zoo animals rushed into their shelters and could not be enticed to come back out.

The belief that wild and domestic animals possess a sixth sense[1]—and know in advance when the earth is going to shake—has been around for centuries.

Wildlife experts believe animals' more acute hearing and other senses might enable them to hear or feel the Earth's vibration, tipping them off[2] to approaching disaster long before humans realize what's going on.

The massive tsunami[3] was triggered by a magnitude 9 temblor[4] off the coast of northern Sumatra island on December 26. The giant waves rolled through the Indian Ocean, killing more than 150,000 people in a dozen countries.

Relatively few animals have been reported dead, however, reviving speculation[5] that animals somehow sense impending disaster.

Ravi Corea, president of the Sri Lanka Wildlife Conservation Society, which is based in Nutley, New Jersey, was in Sri Lanka when the massive waves struck.

Afterward, he traveled to the Patanangala beach inside Yala National Park, where some 60 visitors were washed away.

The beach was one of the worst hit areas of the 500-square-mile (1,300-square-kilometer) wildlife reserve, which is home to a variety of animals, including elephants, leopards, and 130 species of birds.

Corea did not see any animal carcasses nor did the park personnel know of any, other than two water buffaloes that had died, he said.

FOOTNOTES
1 *sixth sense:* knowledge about something before it happens
2 *tipping them off:* giving them a clue
3 *tsunami:* huge ocean waves
4 *magnitude 9 temblor:* an extremely destructive earthquake
5 *speculation:* a guess made without facts

Along India's Cuddalore coast, where thousands of people perished, the Indo-Asian News service reported that buffaloes, goats, and dogs were found unharmed.

Flamingos that breed this time of year at the Point Calimere wildlife sanctuary[6] in India flew to higher ground beforehand, the news service reported.

Strange Animal Behavior

Accounts of strange animal behavior have also started to surface.

About an hour before the tsunami hit, Corea said, people at Yala National Park observed three elephants running away from the Patanangala beach.

World Wildlife Fund, an organization that leads international efforts to protect endangered species and their habitats, has satellite collars[7] on some of the elephants in the park.

A spokeswoman said they plan to track the elephants on that fateful day to verify whether they did move to higher ground. She doesn't know, though, when the satellite data will be downloaded and analyzed.

Corea, a Sri Lankan who emigrated to the United States 20 years ago, said two of his friends noticed unusual animal behavior before the tsunami.

One friend, in the southern Sri Lankan town of Dickwella, recalls bats frantically flying away just before the tsunami struck. Another friend, who lives on the coast near Galle, said his two dogs would not go for their daily run on the beach.

"They are usually excited to go on this outing," Corea said. But on this day they refused to go and most probably saved his life.

Alan Rabinowitz, director for science and exploration at the Bronx Zoo-based Wildlife Conservation Society in New York, says animals can sense impending danger by detecting subtle or abrupt shifts in the environment.

"Earthquakes bring vibrational changes on land and in water while storms cause electromagnetic changes in the atmosphere," he said. "Some animals have acute sense of hearing and smell that allow them to determine something coming towards them long before humans might know that something is there."

FOOTNOTES
....
[6] *sanctuary:* a safe place
[7] *satellite collars:* special collars used to track animals

Did Humans Lose Their Sixth Sense?

At one time humans also had this sixth sense, Rabinowitz said, but lost the ability when it was no longer needed or used.

Joyce Poole is director of the Savanna Elephant Vocalization Project,[8] which has its headquarters in Norway. She has worked with African elephants in Kenya for 25 years. She said the reports of Sri Lanka's elephants fleeing to higher ground didn't surprise her.

Research on both acoustic[9] and seismic[10] communication indicates that elephants could easily pick up vibrations generated from the massive earthquake-tsunami, she said.

Poole has also experienced this firsthand.

"I have been with elephants during two small tremors, and on both occasions the elephants ran in alarm several seconds before I felt the tremor," she said.

One of the world's most earthquake-prone[11] countries is Japan, where devastation has taken countless lives and caused enormous damage to property. Researchers there have long studied animals in hopes of discovering what they hear or feel before the earth shakes. They hope that animals may be used as a prediction tool.

Some U.S. seismologists, on the other hand, are skeptical. There have been documented cases of strange animal behavior prior to earthquakes. But the United States Geological Survey, a government agency that provides scientific information about the Earth, says a reproducible connection between a specific behavior and the occurrence of a quake has never been made.

"What we're faced with is a lot of anecdotes," said Andy Michael, a geophysicist at USGS. "Animals react to so many things—being hungry, defending their territories, mating, predators—so it's hard to have a controlled study to get that advanced warning signal."

In the 1970s a few studies on animal prediction were done by the USGS, "but nothing concrete came out of it," Michael said. Since that time the agency has made no further investigations into the theory.

FOOTNOTES

8 *Savanna Elephant Vocalization Project:* a study of the ways elephants communicate using sound

9 *acoustic:* related to sound or hearing

10 *seismic:* related to vibrations

11 *earthquake-prone:* tends to be affected by earthquakes

Explain Yourself

Answer each question on a separate piece of paper. Be sure to explain your answers.

1. How would you **entice** a mouse to come out of its hole? Explain.

2. If you have an **acute** sense of smell, should you see a doctor? Why or why not?

3. What are some things that can **trigger** an avalanche? Explain.

4. What is one way to **revive** someone? Explain.

5. What would you do if you had an important test **impending**? Why?

6. What would your hometown look like if it was **devastated**? Explain.

7. What kind of **anecdote** would you share with a friend? Explain.

8. If someone is described as **erratic**, how does he or she act? Explain.

9. How would you feel if you finished a race and the final results were **inconclusive**? Why?

10. Is a **portent** something to be afraid of? Why or why not?

VOCABULARY

entice If you entice someone to do something, you get him or her to do it by making it seem appealing.

acute If something is acute, it is sensitive and powerful enough to detect even the smallest change.

trigger If something triggers an event, it makes the event happen.

revive If you revive someone or something, you give it new life or new energy.

impending If something is impending, there are signs that it is about to happen.

devastation Devastation is total, widespread destruction.

anecdote An anecdote is a short, entertaining story about something that has happened.

erratic Something erratic happens in odd, unpredictable patterns.

inconclusive If something is inconclusive, it does not prove anything or comes to no conclusion.

portent A portent is a warning sign that something bad is about to happen.

Take It Further

Complete these sentences on a separate piece of paper.

1. Renee tried to make the meal look **enticing** by . . .

2. A dog's hearing is **acute** enough to . . .

3. The ringing alarm clock **triggered** . . .

4. Maya tried to **revive** her story by . . .

5. Juan's **impending** driving test made him . . .

6. The class was **devastated** to learn that . . .

7. Although Sophia meant the **anecdote** to be . . .

8. Anita **erratically** painted . . .

9. Mr. Walker's heat experiment was **inconclusive**, so . . .

10. Quang thought his dream was a **portent** that . . .

Explore It

One word can take many different forms. Together, these forms make a word family. For example:

entice (verb) = to persuade someone to do something

enticement (noun) = a reward or bonus

enticing (adjective) = something that is tempting

enticingly (adverb) = acting in a tempting way

Working with a partner, write down the different forms of the word *devastate* on a separate piece of paper and discuss the meaning of each. Then act out or illustrate one form of *devastate*. Share your skit or illustration with the class and challenge others to guess which form you used.

HIDDEN MESSAGES

For more than 50 years, people have searched movies and television shows, trying to find "hidden messages." They believe these messages try to entice viewers to buy everything from junk food to cars.

Creating Hidden Messages

Movies and TV programs are made of millions of images. Think of a single photo in a picture frame. Now imagine it changing 30 times in a second! These fast changes are what make characters' actions come alive on TV or in a movie.

Some people believe that inserting one picture or word in a frame every second could cause a "hidden message" to flash across the screen. Because it happens so quickly, the brain wouldn't know it had seen the image.

Using Hidden Messages to Sell Products

In the 1950s, a man named James Vicary came up with the term "subliminal advertising." He used it to describe the idea of using hidden messages to advertise products. He believed his hidden messages were so subtle that even people with very acute senses would not realize that they'd seen the messages. Instead, they would just think that they had a craving for the items advertised.

TOP SECRET

Make Your Own Hidden Messages

Spies have been known to use invisible ink so they can keep their messages a secret. Here's how you can create a secret message.

You will need:
- lemon juice
- a small glass
- toothpicks
- a light bulb (or other heat source)
- paper

Procedure:

1 Soak the point of the toothpick in the juice.

2 Write a message with your toothpick on your paper.

3 Hold the paper over the light bulb but be careful not to touch the light bulb. This will heat your message and make it visible.

The Popcorn and Soda Experiment

In 1957, Vicary tried out his new ads at a movie theater. He said he showed two messages to more than 45,000 people. The ads he flashed read "Eat Popcorn" and "Drink Coca-Cola." During six weeks of testing, Vicary claimed that popcorn and soda sales rose by double digits! However, people soon began to wonder about the test. Had the ads really triggered people to buy the products?

TV and Radio Ban Subliminal Advertising

Many Americans saw hidden messages as an evil portent of technology. Congress believed that Americans should be protected from this kind of advertising. But first, they wanted to find out if Vicary's claims were real.

In 1958, Congress tried to ban subliminal messages. They conducted a study to see how people were affected by the messages. The results were inconclusive. No one could prove that the ads worked.

Rev Up Your Writing

People have different opinions about subliminal advertising. Write a letter to a movie studio persuading them that using hidden messages in movies is either a good idea or bad idea. Use as many of the vocabulary words as possible but make sense.

Word Organizer

Copy this graphic organizer onto a separate piece of paper.

List words or phrases that mean almost the same as *impending* and write your answers in the web. Then tell about a time when something was impending in your life.

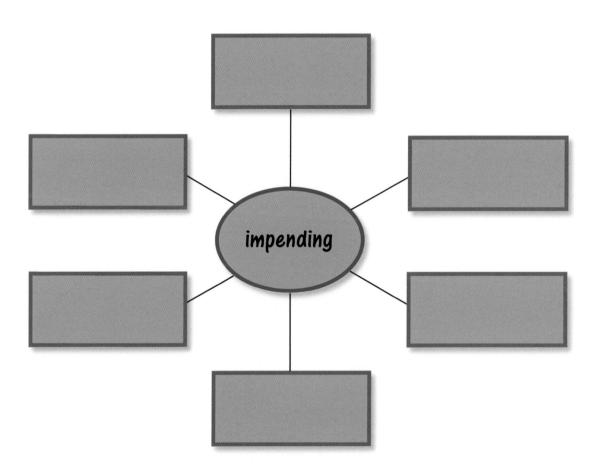

Top 5 Hurricane Myths

1 Storm surges only affect people on the coast.

WRONG! *A storm surge is water driven inland by the powerful hurricane winds. Storm surges can reach 25–30 feet high and can travel for miles.*

2 Hurricanes only affect the side of the house facing the ocean.

WRONG! *Hurricane winds are erratic—they come from all directions, including above.*

3 The worst part of living through a hurricane is the wind.

WRONG! *Most people who are killed by hurricanes die as a result of drowning. The high winds cause some damage, but flooding causes the greatest devastation.*

4 The weather forecasters must have gotten it wrong—the weather is great here.

WRONG! *Hurricanes are very unpredictable. Waiting until you see the impending danger with your own eyes is too late. Trust the forecasters who are using radar to track approaching storms.*

5 Once a hurricane moves over land, it's over.

WRONG! *Hurricanes weaken as they pass over land. But if they move back over warm water, the rise in temperature will revive the storm.*

Weather Jokes

QUESTION 1: What is a hurricane's favorite dance?

QUESTION 2: Why can't hurricanes tell time?

See answers to these jokes on page 42.

The Storm Hag

A Celtic Folktale

Let me tell you a tale, an ancient anecdote from times past, of an old woman who ushered in winter . . .

Long ago, an old woman terrified the peoples of Ireland and Scotland.

She was fearsome. An icy frost covered her long hair. A single eye glared out from her ice-blue face. With just one touch she spread frost that withered all crops. Some said if you listened to the wind howl at night, you could hear her songs enticing sailors to their impending doom.

They believed she created many of Scotland's lakes and mountains when she dropped baskets of rocks into the sea and changed the shape of the earth. She lurked below the surface of the water and called upon the storms.

Each fall she washed her clothes in a great whirlpool of the sea, flung her basket of hailstones across the pastures, and forced the lands into the depths of winter. Some say if you listen carefully, you can hear her songs against the fierce wind and thrashing waves.

Answer 1: The twist!
Answer 2: Their winds move in a counterclockwise direction!

Rev Up Your Writing

You've just read about two forces of nature—one real and one fantasy. Write about a force of nature you have heard about or experienced. Use as many of the vocabulary words as possible but make sense.

Can You Relate?

Copy this graphic organizer onto a separate piece of paper. Match the following words with their related vocabulary word. If a word relates to more than one vocabulary word, explain why.

blighted   If something is blighted, it is damaged or ruined.
capricious   Capricious things change unexpectedly.
chaotic   If the sea is chaotic, it is choppy and moves in many directions at once.
manic   Manic people act in a strange way.
razed   When something is razed, it is torn down or destroyed.

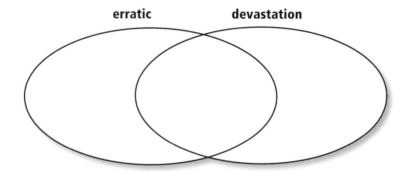

erratic   devastation

In Your Own Words

Respond to one of the following prompts on a separate piece of paper. As you respond, use as many of the vocabulary words as possible. Be creative but make sense!

▶ Write about a time when you experienced chaos in your life. What caused it? How did it happen? What did you learn from this experience?

▶ Write a poem about an animal that does something weird or crazy. What did the animal do? How did others react?

▶ Write about a topic of your choice.

VOCABULARY

entice
acute
trigger
revive
impending
devastation
anecdote
erratic
inconclusive
portent

43

Shooting Lava Rapid

By Will Hobbs

In this exciting account, the narrator and her friends take a dangerous rafting trip through the Grand Canyon. The crew is overwhelmed when they find themselves stuck in the middle of a deadly rapid.

I started pulling hard, digging deep, rowing with my whole body. Pulling, pulling, pulling. With a glance over my shoulder, I saw Troy drifting toward the edge, possibly left of center. It didn't appear that he was going to make it as far left as we'd hoped. If he couldn't get that far over, I knew I couldn't.

With my peripheral vision I saw him disappear. I was still trying to get as far over as I could. Finally, midriver, I reached a place where it was useless to pull against the current. It was sweeping right, and we were on the verge of going over the brink,[1] anyway. I pivoted[2] the boat to face our bow[3] downstream, and I let the current take us.

At last I could see. Just before we went over the edge, I could see that we were going to head down the right side of the tongue.[4] It wasn't where I'd wanted to be. I saw that we were about to drop over a submerged ledge under the brink. It was going to have some snap to it. "Hang on!" I yelled as we went over the edge into the maw of the Thunder.

It was so steep, almost like we were in free fall. I braced for the snap and raised the oar blades high as we dropped into the ledge. I got thrown back by the jolt but held on to the oars and sat upright as we plunged on down the tongue toward the whitewater.[5] As we hit the first whitewater, Star and Adam and the entire front of the boat disappeared in the deluge.

It was all exploding whitewater, towering whitewater, breaking from both sides. My oar blades caught the brunt of the turbulence and my arms flew forward as I instinctively tried to hang on to the oars. My arms would have been yanked from my shoulders if I'd hung on any longer, not that I could. The oars went flying out of control just as a wave from the right broke on me.

I felt myself leaving the raft over the tarped load at the stern. My right hand, clutching desperately behind me, found a strap. In the violence of the water, my body was awash and flying, but I hung on with that one hand. Thrown back down on the load, I found myself flipped onto my stomach.

My free hand found another strap. I'd ended up so far to the back of the raft, my lower legs were out in the river. I knew it was useless to try to climb back over the tarp and scramble for the oars. The boat was already brimful[6] with water and would be impossible to row.

FOOTNOTES

[1] *brink:* the edge of a slope or cliff

[2] *pivoted:* to pivot is to rotate or swing

[3] *bow:* the front part of a boat

[4] *tongue:* a narrow dip between waves

[5] *whitewater:* foamy water seen in rapids

[6] *brimful:* full to the top

If I stayed flat on my stomach, spread-eagled,[7] I had a chance of staying aboard. It was like trying to hang on to the back of a sounding[8] whale.

The bow was pointing directly downriver, as if I were still rowing. I saw it rise up and up onto the first of the mountainous waves in the lower right side of the rapid. Looming high above, its curling crest[9] broke on us. I thought for certain we would flip, but we wallowed through, partly from luck and partly due to the ponderous weight of the water in the raft. I caught a glimpse of Star and Adam floating around in the front of the raft but hanging on with death grips.

We were deluged by torrents[10] and more torrents. It felt like we were underwater, we were being pounded so heavily. Never had I even imagined whitewater on this scale. It was a force of nature all its own, it was a revelation.[11]

Two, three more of these mountains of water broke on us. The last one swept Star out of the raft. She'd floated over the top of the tube, but she was still hanging on. Adam was struggling to resist being floated out himself while working his way over to Star. He managed to haul her back in.

It was only with Lava suddenly behind us and the boat spinning out of control in the whirlpools that I regained the oars. "*Bail!*" I yelled. With a glance downstream I saw Troy's boat right side up. They were screaming at the top of their lungs and so were we.

As soon as the motor rigs saw we were both upright, they took off. We fought for a mile or more to bail out the boats and get to shore. When we finally reached the shore and got the boats tied, we lost it.[12] The six of us just outright lost it, screaming and hugging and falling down in the sand.

46   Lesson 4

Explain Yourself

Answer each question on a separate piece of paper. Be sure to explain your answers.

1. What might a racecar driver see in her **peripheral** vision? Explain.

2. What would you **submerge** in milk? Explain.

3. What animal do you think has the biggest **maw** in the world? Explain.

4. Have you ever experienced a **deluge** of snow? Explain.

5. Would you rather feel the **brunt** of a golf ball or an egg? Explain.

6. Would you say that your mother's birthday is **looming**? Why or why not?

7. Would you expect a good swimmer to **wallow** in the water? Why or why not?

8. Would you move more **ponderously** sledding down a hill or pulling a raft through sand? Explain.

9. What kind of event would make you feel **ecstatic**? Explain.

10. How do you keep your friendships **intact**? Explain.

peripheral Something that is described as being peripheral to something else is on the outer part of it.

submerge Something that is submerged is completely covered by a liquid.

maw A maw is the mouth or jaws of a vicious animal.

deluge A deluge is a large amount of something coming at you all at once, such as a heavy rainstorm.

brunt If you experience the brunt of something, you get the full force or worst part of it.

looming If something is looming over you, it feels like a big and frightening problem.

wallow If you wallow through something, you move through it slowly and with difficulty.

ponderous Something ponderous is heavy and slow moving.

ecstatic If you are ecstatic, you are extremely happy and excited.

intact If something is intact, it is whole and has not been damaged.

Take It Further

Complete these sentences on a separate piece of paper.

1. Gail stored her magazines on the **periphery** of . . .

2. When he started cleaning the house, Barry first **submerged** . . .

3. In the **maw** of the sleeping elephant, researchers found . . .

4. The terrible weather caused a **deluge** of water to . . .

5. The trashcan flew ten feet after receiving the **brunt** of . . .

6. Our good afternoon could be ruined by those **looming** . . .

7. I **wallowed** through the science test, so I . . .

8. The boat trip became **ponderous** after . . .

9. Brenda was **ecstatic** when she found out . . .

10. Pete was amazed that the phone was still **intact** after . . .

LESSON 4
DAY
4

Explore It

Words often have more than one meaning. For example, *wallow* can mean "to move slowly" or "to stay too long in one emotional state."

wallow = "to move slowly"
You might wallow through a muddy, sticky area. If you have to move through something slowly, you have to wallow through it.

> Work with a partner to make a "wallow map" that shows a place where you might wallow and label the features that make travel there so slow.

wallow = "to stay too long in one emotional state"
You might wallow in shame if you embarrassed yourself in front of all of your friends. If you remain too long in one emotional state, you are wallowing.

> Work with a group to write a skit that shows people wallowing in different emotional states.

Rudy Garcia-Tolson:

Taking the "Dis—" out of Disability

By the time Rudy was 5 years old he'd had 15 surgeries. But he still couldn't walk. With another surgery looming, Rudy made a brave decision. He asked the doctors to amputate, or cut off, his legs. If he couldn't walk with legs, he'd learn to walk without them.

With his legs out of the way, Rudy claimed that he was ready to run, jump, and climb trees. The doctors thought Rudy had set his goals too high, but they designed a pair of legs that they thought would allow him to be active.

Rudy's artificial legs were good, but not quite good enough. They kept breaking, and the doctors couldn't figure out why. Rudy's mom explained by showing them a video of her son climbing brick walls and jumping off!

Rudy seemed to have been born without fear. He refused to be disabled. Rudy was faced with a new decision—go easy on the legs, or go tough on the doctors. He convinced the doctors to make him even stronger legs.

Today, Rudy is a world-class athlete. He runs, swims, bikes, and surfs. After looking into the maw of disability and disappointment, Rudy made up his mind. He would live a life of ability and action.

49

Today In *Footvolley*

Vipers No Match for Inferno's Flying Feet

Today was a terrific day for footvolley, a strange cross between beach volleyball and soccer, where players use only their feet, heads, and chests to play volleyball. The crowd cheered wildly when the two teams entered the sand pit. The fans had waited all season to watch the Inferno, great team players, take on the Vipers, the league's most powerful kickers.

The match got off to an exciting start when Inferno team captain, Lorna Sing, kicked the first serve over the net to Andres Pella, who booted the ball into the air, setting up the first Viper score. Janice Holcomb, the other Viper, jumped up and pounded the ball with her feet, zipping it past Sing's head. Sing may have seen the ball in her peripheral vision, but had no time to stop it.

Eventually, the game was tied 14 to 14 with one point needed for a win. Ira Stein served a quick kick to Sing. Sing escaped the brunt of the kicked ball and shot her feet into the air just before it crossed the net. She kicked the ball just right and Inferno's winning point smashed into the sand. With their teamwork intact, the Inferno stayed strong against the powerful Vipers. What a match!

Rev Up Your Writing

You've just read about the experiences people have playing sports. What have you learned from playing sports or doing a physical activity? Use as many of the vocabulary words as possible but make sense.

Word Organizer

Copy this graphic organizer onto a separate piece of paper.

List things and events that make you ecstatic in the top half of the Word Wheel. List things and events that do not make you feel ecstatic in the bottom half.

Yes

No

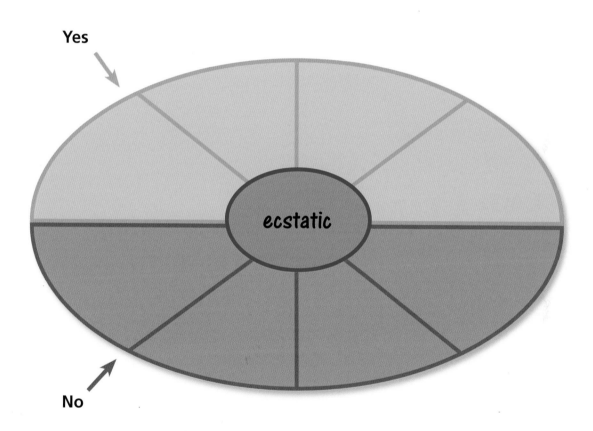

WANTED
Crime Scene Photographer

Do you submerge yourself in detective shows about crime scene investigations? If so, apply for an exciting job as a crime scene photographer with the Rockdale Police Department.

We are looking for people with:
- eyes that can detect the smallest detail
- fantastic photography skills
- the ability to keep even the juiciest details a secret

If this sounds like your dream job, contact the RPD today. We'd be ecstatic to have you join us!

Teen Crime Photographer Helps Solve Burglary Case

ROCKDALE, USA—Using skills she learned as an assistant crime scene photographer, eighteen-year-old Lisa Williams has helped the Rockdale Police Department solve the burglary of a local video game store. Her valuable pictures of the broken door and the stockroom helped detectives figure out what exactly was stolen and how the burglars broke in. Lisa's excellent photographs of the entire store were also helpful in identifying the actual position that evidence was in before a strong wind sent trash flying through the broken door. Thanks to Lisa, the police have returned the stolen games to

Game Warehouse. The store owner, grateful for Lisa's quick thinking, has ecstatically donated brand new games to the local community center.

Evening television is full of exciting programs about crime scene investigators (CSIs). The Rockville Inquirer is lucky to speak with the Rockville Police Department's own CSI, Aldo Alvarado.

CSI: ROCKVILLE

Rockville Inquirer: Aldo, can you tell our readers a little about what a CSI does?

Aldo Alvarado: The first thing a CSI does is go to the scene of the crime and collect the physical evidence.

R.I.: What sort of evidence is that?

Aldo Alvarado: Fingerprints are important. They help identify who has been on the scene. We also make plaster models of tire tracks or footprints. But before anything is touched, our photographer takes pictures of everything. It's a lot of work, but when we are deluged with evidence, we get to the right answer faster.

R.I.: Sounds like a ponderous process. What new research and practices help you with your job?

Aldo Alvarado: The most important advances in murder investigations have come from the information collected by Dr. Bill Bass and his so-called "Body Farm." He's done great research into how a body decomposes, or breaks down, after a person has died.

R.I.: That sounds gross.

Aldo Alvarado: I guess it is, but Dr. Bass' research has kept detectives from wallowing in uncertainty about the cause and time of a person's death. The place is called the "body farm" because Dr. Bass does his experiments in a place with several acres of wooded land rather than in an ordinary lab.

R.I. Well, thanks for all your detailed work, Detective Alvarado. I'll bet the people of Rockville are glad to know you're on the job.

Rev Up Your Writing

You've just read about interesting methods of solving crimes. Write about a time when you or someone you know came up with an unusual way of solving a problem. Use as many of the vocabulary words as possible but make sense.

CROSS

Can You Relate?

Copy this graphic organizer onto a separate piece of paper. Match the following words with their related vocabulary word. If a word relates to more than one vocabulary word, explain why.

apathetic   An apathetic person is not interested or doesn't care.
ardent   Ardent people have very intense feelings about things they like.
languid   Something or someone who is languid seems to never be in a hurry.
melodramatic   Melodramatic people overly exaggerate their emotions.
sluggish   A sluggish person moves very slowly.

wallow	ecstatic	ponderous

In Your Own Words

VOCABULARY

peripheral
submerge
maw
deluge
brunt
looming
wallow
ponderous
ecstatic
intact

Respond to one of the following prompts on a separate piece of paper. As you respond, use as many of the vocabulary words as possible. Be creative but make sense!

▶ Compare two activities you enjoy. Write about how these activities are the same and how they are different. Which one do you like better? Why?

▶ Pretend that you are a crime scene investigator and write a log detailing the scene and what the clues tell you about the crime.

▶ Write about a topic of your choice.

Getups

By Maya Angelou

What does your clothing say about you? Author Maya Angelou doesn't dress to impress others. She dresses to express herself.

I was a twenty-one-year-old single parent with my son in kindergarten. Two jobs allowed me an apartment, food, and child care payment. Little money was left over for clothes, but I kept us nicely dressed in discoveries bought at the Salvation Army and other secondhand shops. Loving colors, I bought for myself beautiful reds and oranges, and greens and pinks, and teals and turquoise. I chose azure[1] dresses and blouses and sweaters. And quite often I wore them in mixtures which brought surprise, to say the least, to the eyes of people who could not avoid noticing me. In fact, I concocted what southern black women used to call "getups."

Because I was very keen that my son not feel that he was neglected or different, I went frequently to his school. Sometimes between my jobs I would just go and stand outside the fenced play area. And he would, I am happy to say, always come and acknowledge me in the colorful regalia.[2] I always wore beads. Lots of beads. The cheaper they were, the more I got, and sometimes I wore head wraps.

When my son was six and I twenty-two, he told me quite solemnly that he had to talk to me. We both sat down at the kitchen table, and he asked with an old man's eyes and a young boy's voice, "Mother, do you have any sweaters that match?" I was puzzled at first. I said, "No," and then I understood he was talking about the pullover and cardigan sets which were popular with white women. And I said, "No, I don't," maybe a little huffily. And he said, "Oh, I wish you did. So that you could wear them to school when you come to see me."

I was tickled, but I am glad I didn't laugh because he continued, "Mother, could you please only come to school when they call you?" Then I realized that my attire, which delighted my heart and certainly activated my creativity, was an embarrassment to him.

When people are young, they desperately need to conform, and no one can embarrass a young person in public so much as an adult to whom he or she is related. Any outré[3] action or wearing of "getups" can make a young person burn with self-consciousness.

FOOTNOTES
. . . .
1 *azure:* light blue
2 *regalia:* ceremonial clothing
3 *outré:* French word meaning bizarre or unusual

I learned to be a little more discreet to avoid causing him displeasure. As he grew older and more confident, I gradually returned to what friends thought of as my eccentric way of dressing. I was happier when I chose and created my own fashion.

I have lived in this body all my life and know it much better than any fashion designer. I think I know what looks good on me, and I certainly know what feels good in me.

I appreciate the creativity which is employed in the design of fabric and the design of clothes, and when something does fit my body and personality, I rush to it, buy it quickly, and wear it frequently. But I must not lie to myself for fashion's sake. I am only willing to purchase the item which becomes me and to wear that which enhances my image of myself to myself.

If I am comfortable inside my skin, I have the ability to make other people comfortable inside their skins although their feelings are not my primary reason for making my fashion choice. If I feel good inside my skin and clothes, I am thus free to allow my body its sway, its natural grace, its natural gesture. Then I am so comfortable that whatever I wear looks good on me even to the external fashion arbiters.[4]

Dress is important to mention because many people are imprisoned by powerful dictates on what is right and proper to wear. Those decisions made by others and sometimes at their convenience are not truly meant to make life better or finer or more graceful or more gracious. Many times they stem from[5] greed, insensitivity, and the need for control.

I have been in company,[6] not long to be sure, but in company where a purveyor[7] of taste will look at a woman or man who enters a room and will say with a sneer, "That was last year's jacket." As hastily as possible, I leave that company, but not before I record the snide attitude which has nothing to do with the beauty or effectiveness of the garment, but rather gives the speaker a moment's sense of superiority at, of course, someone else's expense.

FOOTNOTES

[4] *arbiter:* someone who decides on an issue or influences others

[5] *stem from:* are caused by

[6] *in company:* around people

[7] *purveyor:* person who supplies something

Seek the fashion which truly fits and befits you. You will always be in fashion if you are true to yourself, and only if you are true to yourself. You might, of course, rightly wear that style which is emblazoned on the pages of the fashion magazines of the day, or you might not.

The statement "Clothes make the man" should be looked at, reexamined, and in fact reevaluated. Clothes can make the man or woman look silly and foppish[8] and foolish. Try rather to be so much yourself that the clothes you choose increase your naturalness and grace.

FOOTNOTES
....
[8] *foppish:* caring too much about his or her appearance

Explain Yourself

Answer each question on a separate piece of paper. Be sure to explain your answers.

1. What grade would you get on a report you **concocted**? Explain.

2. What school activity do you do **solemnly**?

3. In what ways does TV encourage people to **conform**?

4. When would a police officer need to be **discreet**?

5. Would you admire someone who lacks **grace**? Why or why not?

6. What **dictate** at your school do you think is the most important to follow?

7. How could you tell if someone was being **snide** toward you?

8. What would you **emblazon** on a t-shirt?

9. What types of movies do you have an **aversion** to?

10. What kind of music would you consider **unconventional**?

concoct   If you concoct something, you make it up on the spot by putting several things together.

solemnly   When you do something solemnly, you do it in a very serious, almost sad way.

conform   If you conform, you make yourself the same as everyone else.

discreet   When people are discreet, they behave in a way that does not draw attention to themselves.

grace   Grace is a smooth, elegant way of doing something.

dictate   A dictate is a rule you have to follow.

snide   Someone who is snide is rude in a sneaky way.

emblazon   When you emblazon something, you display it in a very noticeable way.

aversion   If you have an aversion to something, you really don't like it.

unconventional   Someone or something that is unconventional is different from the usual.

Take It Further

Complete these sentences on a separate piece of paper.

1. Letty **concocted** a milkshake with . . .
2. Huey walked **solemnly** when . . .
3. Vera tried to **conform** because . . .
4. John had to be **discreet** because . . .
5. Dani had so little **grace** that she . . .
6. Janet was upset about the school **dictate** because . . .
7. After hearing the **snide** remark, Todd . . .
8. The hungry family chose the restaurant because it was **emblazoned** with . . .
9. Because Lupe had an **aversion** to flying, she . . .
10. Mila's **unconventional** dress was made from . . .

Explore It

How much do you know about where the words you use came from? Did you know the word *dictate* comes from the word *dictators*? Dictators were judges in ancient Rome who became very powerful during an emergency or disaster. During these dangerous times it was important that everyone follow the rules made by these judges, and breaking the rules could get you into big trouble.

Working with others, research the origin of one of these words. You can use a dictionary, book of word histories, or the Internet. Be ready to present your findings to the class!

1. emperor   2. counselor   3. gladiator   4. senator

She Speaks:

The Growing Voice of African-American Women Poets

Phillis Wheatley

Many people in colonial America made snide comments about the ability of African Americans and women to master the English language. Phillis Wheatley proved them wrong. As a young slave girl she could write as well as any educated scholar, and she did it all on her own.

Shortly after Phillis Wheatley was born, she was sold into slavery, taken from her African homeland, and forced to make the solemn journey to America known as the Middle Passage. Around the age of seven, she became the personal slave of Susannah Wheatley. Unlike most slave owners, the Wheatleys taught Phillis to read. From the beginning it was clear that Phillis was a very talented student. Within a year and a half she could read the entire Bible, and at the age of 12 she began to teach herself Latin. In her teens she traveled to Europe and wrote letters back to her friends in America. In 1773, Phillis wrote *Poems on Various Subjects*, and became the first African-American woman ever to write a published book.

Eventually, Phillis was granted her freedom, and she continued to write poetry throughout her life. Her accomplishments paved the way for all African-American writers.

Gwendolyn Brooks

From an early age, Gwendolyn Brooks had a special gift for writing. However, because her parents stressed her studies so much, she didn't have much time for fun and friends. As a result she grew up very shy. Even after she became a famous poet, she still had an aversion to public life. Her sacrifices and hard work paid off in 1950 when she became the first African American to win the Pulitzer Prize in poetry.

Nikki Giovanni

Nikki Giovanni was always a unique individual. In her first year of college at Fisk University, she was briefly dismissed for her refusal to conform to the school's rules. She was eventually allowed to return to Fisk where she graduated with honors in 1967. Soon after, she started her own publishing company and began to make albums of her poetry spoken over music. She won an award for Best Spoken-Word Album of the Year in 1972, and she has been named "Woman of the Year" by several magazines for her work in literature and civil rights.

Rita Dove

Rita Dove is one of the most famous and respected writers in the world. Her first book of poetry was published in 1980, and only seven years later she won the Pulitzer Prize for poetry. Her greatest achievement came in 1993 when she became the first African American to be named United States Poet Laureate. Despite having her name emblazoned on books of poems and essays, she is still very dedicated to the art of writing.

Rev Up Your Writing

This selection is about the lives and accomplishments of famous poets. Write a poem about a proud or significant moment in your life. Use as many of the vocabulary words as possible but make sense.

Word Organizer

Copy this graphic organizer onto a separate piece of paper.

Write an explanation of the word *emblazon* in the Explain It box below.
Then write a sentence using the word *emblazon* in the Use It box.
Finally, use the Sketch It box to sketch a picture that shows the word
emblazon. Be prepared to explain your work.

emblazon	
Write It	**Explain It**
Use It	**Sketch It**

CRAZY Cars

It is not unusual to see cars painted with bright colors or totally covered with bumper stickers, but outrageous art cars have become a new rage on streets across the country. Have a look at some of the best of these unconventional cars.

PICO DE GALLO

There is no way to be discreet when blasting down the highway in Harrod Blank's Pico de Gallo car. This musical masterpiece sports fender-mounted keyboards, guitars, drums, flutes, and even an accordion. When Blank needs to stage a live concert, he climbs to the disc-shaped platform on the car's roof and grabs a mic. The military-issue speakers on this mariachi-mobile will blow your eardrums and your mind.

THE YARN CAR

Despite rude remarks about grandmothers and knitting, Tim Klein is often praised for the graceful design that he created with four miles of yarn. The designs represent the elements—fire, water, wind, and soil—all of which could do this car some major damage. Tim admits that his car unravels from time to time, but that just gives him a chance to create an even better design.

THE PLAIDMOBILE

When New Jersey's Division of Motor Vehicles required that Tim McNally declare a single color for his car, McNally ignored the dictate. His car could only be described as plaid. He'd spent more than a year designing and painting his car, and there was no way he was going to call it red. After all, this is a guy who regularly wears plaid suits.

Rev Up Your Writing

If you had a car, what kind of art would you use to express yourself? Describe your car in detail and explain why you chose that kind of art. Use as many of the vocabulary words as possible but make sense.

Can You Relate?

Copy this graphic organizer onto a separate piece of paper. Match the following words with their related vocabulary word. If a word relates to more than one vocabulary word, explain why.

dogmatic   Dogmatic people are convinced that they are right, and they will not consider other opinions.

iconoclast   Iconoclasts want to change or completely stop doing things that have been done for a long time.

inhibition   An inhibition is a feeling that stops you from doing something.

radical   If something is radical, it is extremely different or more complex than anything else.

spartan   A spartan way of life is very simple and has no luxuries.

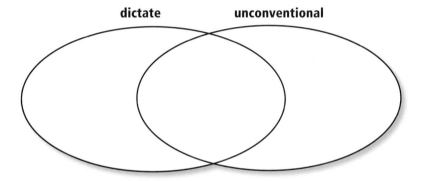
dictate   unconventional

In Your Own Words

Respond to one of the following prompts on a separate piece of paper. As you respond, use as many of the vocabulary words as possible. Be creative but make sense!

▶ Write about a time when you or someone you know did something unique or unconventional. What happened? How did other people react?

▶ People make art out of old bottles, used pizza boxes, and toothpaste. Is this really art, or just junk? Take a side and convince someone to buy or not buy this type of art.

▶ Write about a topic of your choice.

VOCABULARY

concoct
solemnly
conform
discreet
grace
dictate
snide
emblazon
aversion
unconventional

TRUE GRIT

The Stories of Bethany Hamilton & Jim Abbott

Bethany Hamilton overcomes a tragic shark attack and becomes a professional surfer. Like Bethany, Jim Abbott refuses to let his disability keep him from living his dream.

from ExtremeSports360.com

Bethany Hamilton: a Surfer Worth Watching

Bethany Hamilton is one of those rare athletes that has found the courage to prevail where others have failed. Despite having a disadvantage unfairly imposed on her, she has managed to grit her teeth[1] and get on with the game. That is what it's all about. . . .

Bethany Hamilton (born February 8, 1990) is a Hawaiian surfer who is best known for having only one arm. Having survived a shark attack in 2003, in which she lost her left arm, she has made a respectable comeback as a surfer, and has courageously fought to keep the tragedy from debilitating her.

Born in North Shore, Kauai, she learned surfing from her parents, who had moved to Hawaii to be near the big waves in the first place. Learning to surf before she could walk meant she was ahead of her game[2] from the start. At the age of four she won her first competition, and again at the age of seven.

February 2002 saw her take victory at the Haleiwa Menehune Championships, showing up[3] both the under-13s, under-17s and under-12 boys by taking all three titles! Plans to go pro[4] did not take long to formulate.

But, as is so often the case, the world threw her a challenge.[5] On October 31, 2003, Hamilton, best friend Alana Blanchard, Alana's father, Holt, and Alana's brother paddled out into the surf of Tunnels Beach, Hawaii.

The tiger shark came quick, and unexpectedly. Attacking 43cm of the left side of her board and ripping her arm free above the shoulder in one instant, the 4.3 meter monster changed her life forever. Bethany managed to make it to shore despite losing 70% of her blood.

Just 10 weeks after the trauma, Hamilton got back on a custom made[6] board, making it easier to paddle and balance. She was back in the competition in no time.

FOOTNOTES

[1] *grit her teeth:* to work hard to succeed
[2] *ahead of her game:* ahead of others
[3] *showing up:* doing better than
[4] *go pro:* become a professional
[5] *threw her a challenge:* gave her a difficult test
[6] *custom made:* made just for her

"When I got up on my first wave, I rode it all the way into the shore, and after that, I just had, like, tears of happiness," she said. "I was so stoked[7] to be back out there."

As of 2005, Hamilton is still on her way to becoming a professional surfer. The author of a tale widely accepted as courageous, Hamilton says that the incident was a blessing in disguise.[8] She is glad to be an inspiration to others.

In 2004 Bethany won the ESPY Award for Best Comeback Athlete of the Year, and later took a special courage award at the 2004 Teen Choice Awards. She has traveled all over to appear on TV shows and receive awards.

Bethany has written a book about her life called *Soul Surfer*.

FOOTNOTES

[7] *stoked:* excited

[8] *blessing in disguise:* a bad situation that turns into a good one

How to Play Baseball With One Hand

By Jim Abbott

I was born without my right hand. I have never felt slighted. As a kid I was pretty coordinated, and growing up I loved sports. I learned to play baseball like most kids, playing catch with my Dad in the front yard. The only difference was that we had to come up with a method to throw and catch with the same hand. What we came up with is basically what I continued to do my whole life.

I receive letters all the time asking me to describe how to switch the glove from one hand to the other in order to play baseball with just one hand. Let me say right off the bat,[1] there is no right way or wrong way. I learned to switch the glove off and on with my Dad when I was 4 years old and gradually made adjustments. Everybody has different circumstances so it takes a little creative thinking and adjustability. Try everything, find what seems most natural to you. Once you think you've developed a method, just keep practicing and practicing and practicing some more, until switching the glove off and on becomes second nature,[2] almost like tying your shoes.

I used to throw balls against the side of my family's house, pretending to be my favorite pitchers. When the balls bounced off the wall I had to get my glove on incredibly fast if I didn't want to chase those balls down the street all day! I would recommend a rubber coated ball for this method!

As for holding a bat and hitting, it is a very similar process of finding what is the most natural motion for you. I always went with the method that felt the most comfortable to me. For example, some people said I should have hit right handed; well, left handed just seemed more of a natural fit to me. I always wanted to incorporate both arms as best I could. This way felt more balanced to me and more powerful. So I stuck with it.[3] (I did get 2 hits in the majors,[4] although I won't mention my average!)

FOOTNOTES
....
[1] *right off the bat:* right away
[2] *second nature:* something done without thought
[3] *stuck with it:* didn't give up
[4] *majors:* major leagues, in baseball

It is unquestionably a process of trial and error. Whatever you do though, don't give up. Don't let anyone discourage you from believing what you can accomplish. I have been so fortunate to meet so many kids, all over the country, who devised ways of playing baseball that you wouldn't imagine! They were just so determined to play and they loved the game so much they came up with their own methods to help them do it well. In the end, I guess that's my best advice to you—find what it is in life that you love and go after it with all of your heart. I promise, if you have that passion, you will find a way to do what needs to be done. There is nothing that can hold you back!

Explain Yourself

Answer each question on a separate piece of paper. Be sure to explain your answers.

1. If you were a teacher, what rules would you **impose**?

2. Would having extremely long fingernails be **debilitating**? Explain.

3. Would you feel **slighted** if you were chosen to enter an art contest? Why or why not?

4. How would you **incorporate** the talents of all your friends into a business?

5. What kind of plan would you **devise** to earn cash for the weekend? Why?

6. What is the most **appalling** food you have ever heard of? Why?

7. Would you be **adroit** at teaching a person sign language or a foreign language? Explain.

8. What have you done that is **meritorious**? Explain.

9. Would you need to have **fortitude** to swim with sharks? Explain.

10. What would **impede** your attendance at school? Why?

VOCABULARY

impose   When you impose something on people, you force it on them.

debilitate   If a problem debilitates you, it weakens you so that you are unable to live your life in a normal way.

slighted   If you feel slighted, you feel left out or looked down upon.

incorporate   If you incorporate things, you include them or bring them together.

devise   When you devise a way to do something, you invent a creative way of doing it.

appalling   Something that is appalling is horrifying, shocking, or frightening.

adroit   If you are adroit, you are skillful and clever, especially in difficult situations.

meritorious   Someone or something that is meritorious deserves praise and honor.

fortitude   A person who has fortitude faces danger or pain with calm bravery.

impede   If something impedes you, it gets in your way or makes things more difficult for you.

Take It Further

Complete these sentences on a separate piece of paper.

1. A weak leader will **impose** . . .

2. The loss of my toenail was **debilitating** because . . .

3. Joanna felt **slighted** during the party, because . . .

4. The artist **incorporated** . . .

5. Kesha **devised** a way to make her wheelchair . . .

6. Your teacher would probably be **appalled** if . . .

7. A cat is especially **adroit** at . . .

8. My aunt is one of the most **meritorious** people I know because she . . .

9. Zookeepers show great **fortitude** when . . .

10. The crowd **impeded** traffic by . . .

Explore It

Words often have more than one meaning. For example, the word *slight* can mean "a small degree or amount," or it can mean "ignore."

slight = a small degree or amount
A person who is small in size might be described as being slight.
Sometimes it can be easy to overlook someone who is small in size.

> Write a short story about a 13-year-old boy who is very slight for his age. In your story, describe how the boy uses his size to his advantage. Use the word *slight* in your story.

slight = ignore
Sometimes people slight others because they are different. When people slight you, they ignore you or treat you rudely.

> Think about how it might feel to be slighted by a friend. Work with a partner to create a short skit about what happens when one friend slights another. Use the word *slight* in your play.

Say What?!

Adults have long been appalled by teen slang. But just listen to these adults—they use plenty of slang themselves. Slang has been around for as long as people have had the creativity to devise new ways of expressing themselves.

1920s **fire extinguisher:** a chaperone who imposes on you and your date

1930s **bumping your gums:** talking just to talk

1940s **togged to the bricks:** all dressed up

1950s **trying to razz my berries:** trying to impress me

1960s **it's a bummer:** it's depressing

Strong Slang!

Some slang words have great fortitude. Take for example, the following:

"That's cool!" In the 1940s people referred to great things as *cool!*

"That's crazy, Dude!" *Dude* has been used to refer to any man since the 1960s.

"Oh Baby, I love you!" In the 1920s sweethearts called each other "baby."

1970s
catch you on the flip side: see you later (refers to the other side of a vinyl record)

1980s
wannabe: someone who aspires to be something but doesn't quite make it

1990s
trippin': acting unusual or strange

2000s
bling: flashy jewelry

That's Awesome!

Every generation has found new ways to say *good*. Here are some common ways.

1920s—cat's meow
1940s—cool
1950s—crazy
1960s—groovy
1970s—boss
1980s—tubular
1990s—phat

Don't feel slighted. This millennium will have slang words that will last a lifetime. Can you predict which ones?

Rev Up Your Writing

What can slang tell you about others? How does it help you communicate with your friends and family? Explain. Use as many of the vocabulary words as possible but make sense.

Word Organizer

Copy this graphic organizer onto a separate piece of paper.

Impose is near the hot end of the Word-O-Meter. Think of words that would be hotter or colder. Write your answers in the boxes. Explain your answers.

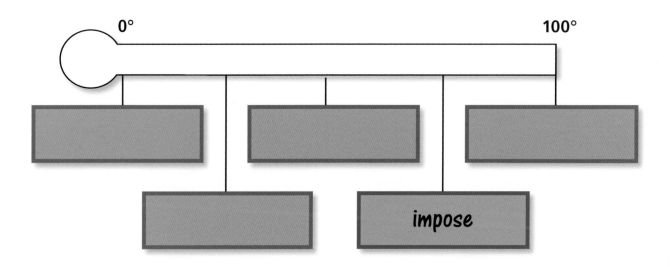

impose

Q: What kind of music might a sad landscaper impose on you?

A: Bluegrass!

e-V☺cabulary

In this totally connected information age, where blogging, texting, IMing, and e-mailing are often chosen over snail mail and face-to-face conversations, the World Wide Web gives you a way to communicate with people on the other side of the planet. By incorporating the use of numbers, pictures, and symbols into your messages, you are using a sort of international slang that is unique to e-culture.

Read the following messages. Are any of these "words" a part of your e-vocabulary?

Dad

IneztheGr8

MyTMIkE

User   **The PerezFam**   **?**

Chat Room   **10:15 AM**

Dad: We really need to get things going for Mom's birthday. ☺

IneztheGr8: Yeah, her b-day is in two weeks, and I have no clue what to get her. Mikey, are you there?

MyTMIkE: SUP y'all?! I'm here. Maybe we can just take her out to dinner and give her a card . . .

IneztheGr8: (@@), right?! IsTHtTBstUCanDo? 😮

MyTMIkE: What's wrong with that??

Dad: C'mon, Mikey—you can do better than that. You must agree that she deserves the meritorious mother of the year award.

MyTMIkE: Yeah . . . you're right. She is pretty terrific, huh? 😃

IneztheGr8: Absolutely. Remember when I was suffering from that debilitating throat disease? She never left the hospital. I was practically dying, and she nursed me back to health.

MyTMIkE: Plz! ROFL! You had your tonsils taken out, for crying out loud! You weren't dying! Don't be such a DrmaQEN!!!

IneztheGr8: LOL! Hey—I couldn't talk for a week! And who are you calling a DrmaQEN, you DrkbrAN BOnhead! ;t

:) | Send

Dad: That's enough! You two are impeding our planning.

MyTMIkE: Sorry.

IneztheGr8: I have an idea. We should give her a total makeover. Then we can put our monE together and treat her to the spa for a day. While she's away, Aunt Tina can help us make over Mom's home office. But we will have to move fast . . .

MyTMIkE: Yo—a total makeover—that rocks! She'll love it! I'll get started painting a few new pictures . . .

Dad: :^D!!! I'll call Aunt Tina. Inez, d:-)! You're so adroit. You always come up with the best ideas in the nick of time!

IneztheGr8: Gee thanks, Dad. GTG. We'll talk more l8r.

MyTMIkE: L8r

Dad: BBFN (((H)))

▶   :) **Send**

e-Vocabulary Glossary

SUP	What's up?
(@@)	You're kidding
IsTHtTBstUCanDo . . .	Is that the best you can do?
DrmaQEN	drama queen
DrkbrAN	dorkbrain
BOnhead	bonehead
;t	pouting
monE	money
:^D	I like it!
d:-)	Hats off to your great idea!
ROFL	rolling on the floor laughing
LOL	laughing out loud
L8r	later (or goodbye)
BBFN	bye bye for now
GTG	got to go
(((H)))	lots of hugs

IneztheGr8

Rev Up Your Writing

How has technology changed the way people communicate today? Explain. Use as many vocabulary words as possible but make sense.

Can You Relate?

Copy this graphic organizer onto a separate piece of paper. Match the following words with their related vocabulary word. If a word relates to more than one vocabulary word, explain why.

hindrance   A hindrance is someone or something that gets in your way.
impeccable   Something that is impeccable is excellent and has no flaws.
impious   If something is impious, it is wicked and evil.
stature   A person's stature is his or her level of achievement.
unsavory   If something is unsavory, it is unwanted or unpleasant.

appalling	impede	meritorious

In Your Own Words

Respond to one of the following prompts on a separate piece of paper. As you respond, use as many of the vocabulary words as possible. Be creative but make sense!

▶ Write about a person who has inspired you. Describe the person and his or her accomplishments.

▶ Write a news article set in the future about a newly invented form of communication. Explain how it was invented and how it will change people's lives.

▶ Write about a topic of your choice.

VOCABULARY

impose
debilitate
slighted
incorporate
devise
appalling
adroit
meritorious
fortitude
impede

He-y, Come On Ou-t!

By Shinichi Hoshi
Illustrated by Cynthia Watts Clark

After a typhoon hits a small village, the villagers go out to inspect the damage from the storm. They soon discover a mysterious, apparently bottomless hole in the ground.

The typhoon[1] had passed and the sky was a gorgeous blue. Even a certain village not far from the city had suffered damage. A little distance from the village and near the mountains, a small shrine[2] had been swept away by a landslide.

"I wonder how long that shrine's been there."

"Well, in any case, it must have been here since an awfully long time ago."

"We've got to rebuild it right away."

While the villagers exchanged views, several more of their number came over.

"It sure was wrecked."

"I think it used to be right here."

"No, looks like it was a little more over there."

Just then one of them raised his voice. "Hey what in the world is this hole?"

Where they had all gathered there was a hole about a meter in diameter. They peered in, but it was so dark nothing could be seen. However, it gave one the feeling that it was so deep it went clear through to the center of the earth.

There was even one person who said, "I wonder if it's a fox's hole."

"He—y, come on ou—t!" shouted a young man into the hole. There was no echo from the bottom. Next he picked up a pebble and was about to throw it in.

"You might bring down a curse on us. Lay off,"[3] warned an old man, but the younger one energetically threw the pebble in. As before, however, there was no answering response from the bottom. The villagers cut down some trees, tied them with rope and made a fence which they put around the hole. Then they repaired[4] to the village.

"What do you suppose we ought to do?"

"Shouldn't we build the shrine up just as it was over the hole?"

A day passed with no agreement. The news traveled fast, and a car from the newspaper company rushed over. In no time a scientist came out, and with an all-knowing expression on his face he went over to the hole. Next, a bunch of gawking[5] curiosity seekers showed up; one could also pick out here and there men of shifty glances who appeared to be concessionaires.[6] Concerned that someone might fall into the hole, a policeman from the local substation kept a careful watch.

FOOTNOTES

[1] *typhoon:* a type of tropical storm
[2] *shrine:* a place where people go to worship
[3] *lay off:* stop doing something
[4] *repaired:* returned
[5] *gawking:* staring hard
[6] *concessionaires:* vendors, salespeople

One newspaper reporter tied a weight to the end of a long cord and lowered it into the hole. A long way down it went. The cord ran out, however, and he tried to pull it out, but it would not come back up. Two or three people helped out, but when they all pulled too hard, the cord parted at the edge of the hole. Another reporter, a camera in hand, who had been watching all of this, quietly untied a stout rope that had been wound around his waist.

The scientist contacted people at his laboratory and had them bring out a high-powered bull horn,[7] with which he was going to check out the echo from the hole's bottom. He tried switching through various sounds, but there was no echo. The scientist was puzzled, but he could not very well give up with everyone watching him so intently. He put the bull horn right up to the hole, turned it to its highest volume, and let it sound continuously for a long time. It was a noise that would have carried several dozen kilometers above ground. But the hole just calmly swallowed up the sound.

In his own mind the scientist was at a loss,[8] but with a look of apparent composure he cut off the sound and, in a manner suggesting that the whole thing had a perfectly plausible[9] explanation, said simply, "Fill it in."

Safer to get rid of something one didn't understand.

The onlookers, disappointed that this was all that was going to happen, prepared to disperse. Just then one of the concessionaires, having broken through the throng[10] and come forward, made a proposal.

"Let me have that hole. I'll fill it in for you."

"We'd be grateful to you for filling it in," replied the mayor of the village, "but we can't very well give you the hole. We have to build a shrine there."

"If it's a shrine you want, I'll build you a fine one later. Shall I make it with an attached meeting hall?"

Before the mayor could answer, the people of the village all shouted out.

"Really? Well, in that case, we ought to have it closer to the village."

"It's just an old hole. We'll give it to you!"

So it was settled. And the mayor, of course, had no objection.

The concessionaire was true to his promise. It was small, but closer to the village he did build for them a shrine with an attached meeting hall.

FOOTNOTES

[7] *bull horn:* a cone-shaped machine used to make one's voice louder

[8] *at a loss:* puzzled or unable to explain something

[9] *plausible:* believable

[10] *throng:* a large crowd

About the time the autumn festival was held at the new shrine, the hole-filling company established by the concessionaire hung out its small shingle[11] at a shack near the hole.

The concessionaire had his cohorts[12] mount a loud campaign in the city. "We've got a fabulously deep hole! Scientists say it's at least five thousand meters deep! Perfect for the disposal of such things as waste from nuclear reactors."

Government authorities granted permission. Nuclear power plants fought for contracts. The people of the village were a bit worried about this, but they consented when it was explained that there would be absolutely no above-ground contamination for several thousand years and that they would share in the profits. Into the bargain, very shortly a magnificent road was built from the city to the village.

Trucks rolled in over the road, transporting lead boxes. Above the hole lids were opened, and the wastes from nuclear reactors tumbled away into the hole.

From the Foreign Ministry and the Defense Agency boxes of unnecessary classified documents were brought for disposal. Officials who came to supervise the disposal held discussions on golf. The lesser functionaries,[13] as they threw in the papers, chatted about pinball.

The hole showed no signs of filling up. It was awfully deep, thought some; or else it might be very spacious at the bottom. Little by little the hole-filling company expanded its business.

Bodies of animals used in contagious disease experiments at the universities were brought out, and to these were added the unclaimed corpses of vagrants. Better than dumping all of its garbage in the ocean, went the thinking in the city, and plans were made for a long pipe to carry it to the hole.

The hole gave peace of mind[14] to the dwellers of the city. They concentrated solely on producing one thing after another. Everyone disliked thinking about the eventual consequences. People wanted only to work for production companies and sales corporations; they had no interest in becoming junk dealers. But, it was thought, these problems too would gradually be resolved by the hole.

FOOTNOTES
. . . .
[11] *hung out its small shingle:* gave public notice that the office was opening
[12] *cohorts:* partners
[13] *lesser functionaries:* less-important government employees
[14] *peace of mind:* a feeling of calm and relaxation

Young girls whose betrothals[15] had been arranged discarded old diaries in the hole. There were also those who were inaugurating new love affairs and threw into the hole old photographs of themselves taken with former sweethearts. The police felt comforted as they used the hole to get rid of accumulations of expertly done counterfeit bills. Criminals breathed easier after throwing material evidence[16] into the hole.

Whatever one wished to discard, the hole accepted it all. The hole cleansed the city of its filth; the sea and sky seemed to have become a bit clearer than before. Aiming at the heavens, new buildings went on being constructed one after the other.

One day, atop the high steel frame of a new building under construction, a workman was taking a break. Above his head he heard a voice shout:

"He—y, come on ou—t!"

But, in the sky to which he lifted his gaze there was nothing at all. A clear blue sky merely spread over all. He thought it must be his imagination. Then, as he resumed his former position, from the direction where the voice had come, a small pebble skimmed by him and fell on past.

The man, however, was gazing in idle reverie at the city's skyline growing ever more beautiful, and he failed to notice.

FOOTNOTES
[15] *betrothals:* plans to marry
[16] *material evidence:* important clues in a case

Explain Yourself

Answer each question on a separate piece of paper. Be sure to explain your answers.

1. Which sports are usually played by **stout** athletes? Why?

2. If a crowd of people at the movies **disperses**, what has probably happened? Explain.

3. If a friend asked to borrow your favorite CD, would you **consent**? Why or why not?

4. What is one object you'd never **discard**? Why?

5. How might you **inaugurate** a new school year? Explain.

6. Are you likely to be lost in a **reverie** at a funeral? Why or why not?

7. What can you do to **irrevocably** damage a computer? Explain.

8. What might make a fieldtrip feel **interminable**? Explain.

9. What would happen if you used **noxious** berries to make a pie? Why?

10. What are some **ramifications** of putting off your homework until the last minute? Explain.

VOCABULARY

stout   Someone or something that is stout is strong, thick, and heavy for its size.

disperse   When something disperses, it breaks apart and scatters in different directions.

consent   When you consent to something, you agree to do it or to let it be done.

discard   When you discard something, you throw it away or get rid of it.

inaugurate   When you inaugurate something, you officially begin it.

reverie   A reverie is a long daydream full of pleasant thoughts.

irrevocable   An action that is irrevocable cannot be undone or revoked.

interminable   If something is interminable, it seems like it's taking forever.

noxious   A noxious substance will damage your health and may kill you.

ramification   If some action has ramifications, there are possible consequences that you might not have thought of.

Take It Further

Complete these sentences on a separate piece of paper.

1. The tree branch wasn't **stout** enough to . . .

2. The students started to **disperse** when . . .

3. After hours of discussion, my parents finally **consented** to . . .

4. Susannah **discarded** Austin's poem because . . .

5. To **inaugurate** the summer, our family . . .

6. Jacqi fell into a **reverie** about . . .

7. When the teacher said her decision to cancel the field trip was **irrevocable**, we . . .

8. The car ride seemed **interminable**, so I . . .

9. When scientists found **noxious** liquids in the river, they . . .

10. We didn't realize the **ramifications** of staying up all night would be . . .

Explore It

How much do you know about where the words you use come from? For example, did you know that the word *inaugurate* comes from an old Roman tradition? In ancient Rome, officials called *augurs* made predictions about important events by watching birds. That's why the Latin word *inaugurare* means "to give power to a leader after consulting the birds." These days, we don't usually consult birds before choosing our leaders, but our word *inauguration* comes from this tradition.

Working with others, research the origin of one of your vocabulary words using a dictionary, book of word origins, or the Internet. Be ready to present your findings to the class!

Ask AUNTIE GIZMO

Dear Auntie Gizmo,
My puppy, Gogo, keeps running away. I want to take him places, but I'm worried that he'll get lost. How can I get him out of the house but keep him close?
—Doggone Worried in Detroit

Dear Doggone,
You and Gogo will travel in safety and style with the Wearable Dog House! It's a flexible compartment for your pooch that you can strap over your shoulders and wear on your front or back. Keep Gogo close to you at all times and impress your friends with your unique outfit. When you see Wearable Dog Houses on the fashion runways of New York and Europe, you can say your Auntie Gizmo told you about them first.

Dear Auntie Gizmo,
I'm going to a family reunion, but my cousins are sick and I'm worried about catching a cold. Help!
—Sneezy in Sacramento

Dear Sneezy,
Why not let Kissing Shields protect you from those no-good germs? Each Kissing Shield is made of a plastic sheet stretched over a heart-shaped frame. Just hold one in front of your lips before consenting to kiss Grandma Celeste, discard it, and grab another before greeting Uncle Rodney. Thanks to its heart shape, the Kissing Shield is also perfect for Valentine's Day.

Dear Auntie Gizmo,
Sometimes the school day feels interminable. How can I make classes go by faster?
—Tick Tock in Tuscaloosa

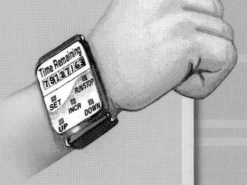

Dear Tick,
You should get your hands on a Life Expectancy Watch. This brilliant timepiece will count down the years, days, hours, minutes, and seconds until your personal death day. Think how slowly you'll want each class to go—instead of thinking, "40 minutes to freedom," you'll be saying, "Only 75 years left!"

The GREAT Invention

I've done it! I've invented the greatest new machine
since TV or the telephone: a robot that can clean!
I've always hated tidying my room and raking leaves,
so I have made my robots love cleaning up for me.

They'll dust the sandwich crumbs away as I lounge in my chair.
I'll munch in blissful reverie while robots comb my hair.
They'll clutch a fluffy dishcloth in their strong metallic hands;
they'll polish all the silverware and organize the pans.

But here's the best part: when the robots make everything shine,
I'll show their work to Mom and Dad and say that it was mine.
They'll give me my allowance—a truly brilliant trick
with no ramifications, and I'm sure I'll get rich quick!

The only catch is that the robots need to clean like me,
so I have made my robots just as human as can be.
My parents won't be able to see differences between
their work and mine—a perfect blend of human and machine.

It's time to ask my robots to start on their first task
of folding all the laundry while I sit back and relax.
But wait! What's happening? My plan has worked too well!
My robots are too human. It's too horrible to tell!

They're lying on the sofa and reading magazines,
and leaving crumbs all over from their grilled cheese!
Since my robots won't clean, well then I guess
I'll have to be the one who cleans up the mess!

Rev Up Your Writing

You've read about a few strange inventions. Draw a wacky invention of your own, and then write about what it does and who would use it. Use as many of the vocabulary words as possible but make sense.

Word Organizer

Copy this graphic organizer onto a separate piece of paper.

List things that people usually discard in the top half of the Word Wheel. List things that aren't usually discarded in the bottom half.

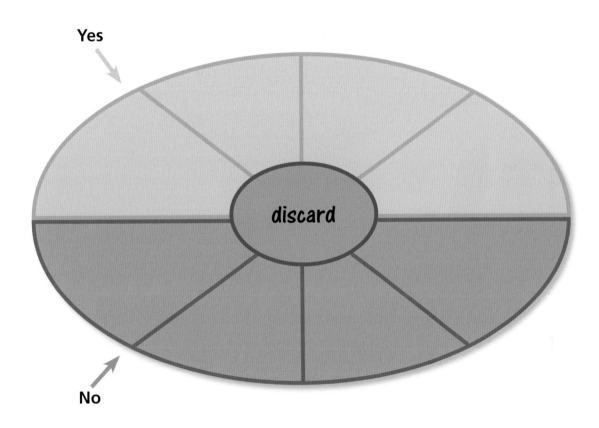

It's a Car! It's a Fridge!
It's . . . Stonehenge?

Ever heard of Stonehenge? It's an ancient circle of standing stones in a field in England. It's also home to a lot of mysteries. Who built it? What was its purpose? And why has someone built a copy of it using old cars?

Stonehenge Version 1.0

It probably won't surprise you to learn that the real Stonehenge is made of giant stones, not cars. Most people think Stonehenge is about 5,000 years old, but no one really knows why it was built. Some people think ceremonies were performed at Stonehenge. Others think Stonehenge was used to study the sun. Nobody knows much about this mysterious place. That doesn't stop tourists from traveling hundreds of miles to see it though!

A Fine Fake: Foamhenge

While the original Stonehenge may be neat to see, Foamhenge is probably a whole lot closer to home. It's set on a hill in Virginia's Blue Ridge Mountains, and most of it was built in just one day! That's probably because styrofoam is a little easier to move than massive stones. The first version blew down after only three months; to make sure that his creation was irrevocable, Foamhenge's creator went back and used stouter foam and anchored each block into concrete. Since this foam is nonbiodegradable, Foamhenge could last longer than the original!

A Chill Destination: Stonefridge

Lots of Stonehenge look-alikes are dispersed across the United States. Some of them, like Foamhenge, look almost like the original, but some are downright wacky! For example, New Mexico is home to Stonefridge, a monument made of over 200 stout refrigerators. It may not be as old as Stonehenge, but it's almost as mysterious. And it's definitely cool.

Honk if You Love Carhenge

If you think foam and refrigerators are the only things you can use to build zany Stonehenges, think again! Check out Nebraska's Carhenge. It's a circle of 38 cars arranged to look like Stonehenge. Originally built as a memorial, it was inaugurated in 1987. At first, people who lived near Carhenge wanted to tear it down. They thought it was a noxious pile of junk! Now Carhenge is a popular tourist spot, sort of like the real Stonehenge.

These modern Stonehenges may seem silly, but who knows? In thousands of years, people may visit Carhenge or Stonefridge, stare in wonder, and try to uncover their mysteries.

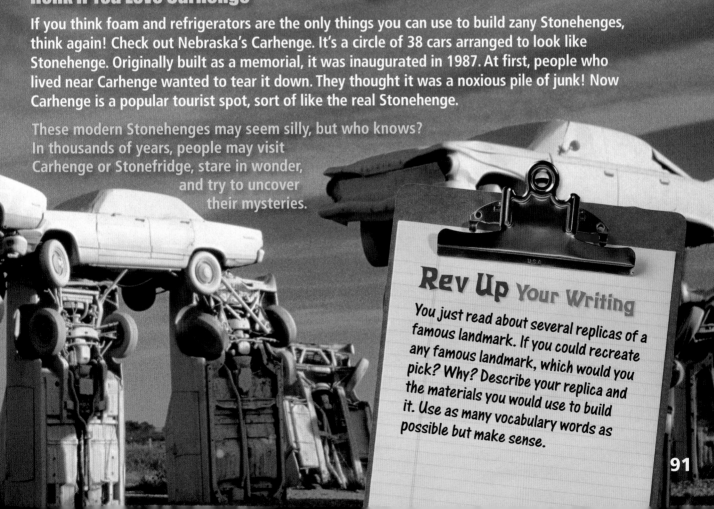

Rev Up Your Writing

You just read about several replicas of a famous landmark. If you could recreate any famous landmark, which would you pick? Why? Describe your replica and the materials you would use to build it. Use as many vocabulary words as possible but make sense.

Can You Relate?

Copy this graphic organizer onto a separate piece of paper. Match the following words with their related vocabulary word. If a word relates to more than one vocabulary word, explain why.

aftermath The aftermath of an important event is what happens as a result of it.

concede If you concede something, you give in and agree to it.

ensuing An ensuing event happens right after something else.

license If you have license to do something, you have freedom or permission to do it.

rueful Someone who is rueful feels regret for something he or she did.

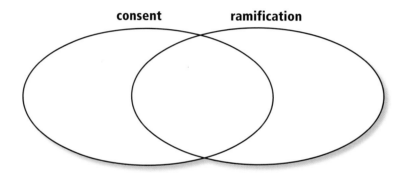

consent   ramification

In Your Own Words

Respond to one of the following prompts on a separate piece of paper. As you respond, use as many of the vocabulary words as possible. Be creative but make sense!

▶ Write about a time when you or someone you know did something that had consequences you didn't expect. What did you do? What were the consequences? What did you learn from this experience?

▶ You've made an amazing discovery that will change your whole town. Write a letter to the head of your town describing what you've found and explaining why it's important.

▶ Write about a topic of your choice.

VOCABULARY

stout
disperse
consent
discard
inaugurate
reverie
irrevocable
interminable
noxious
ramification

Identity

By Julio Noboa Polanco

Would you dare to be different if it meant not being accepted by others? In this poem, the speaker tries to answer this question by comparing the life of a weed to the life of a flower.

Let them be as flowers,
always watered, fed, guarded, admired,
but harnessed to a pot of dirt.

I'd rather be a tall, ugly weed,
clinging on cliffs, like an eagle
wind-wavering above high, jagged rocks.

To have broken through the surface of stone
to live, to feel exposed[1] to the madness
of the vast, eternal sky.
To be swayed by the breezes of an ancient sea,
carrying my soul, my seed beyond the mountains of time
or into the abyss of the bizarre.

I'd rather be unseen, and if,

then shunned by everyone
than to be a pleasant-smelling flower,
growing in clusters in the fertile[2] valley
where they're praised, handled, and plucked
by greedy, human hands.

I'd rather smell of musty, green stench
than of sweet, fragrant lilac.[3]
If I could stand alone, strong and free,
I'd rather be a tall, ugly weed.

FOOTNOTES

[1] *exposed:* open or uncovered

[2] *fertile:* able to support and produce growth

[3] *lilac:* a flower known for its pleasant smell

Explain Yourself

Answer each question on a separate piece of paper. Be sure to explain your answers.

1. What kinds of animals are typically **harnessed**? Explain.

2. If you were sure of what you wanted, would you **waver**? Why or why not?

3. When would a day feel **eternal**? Explain.

4. What kinds of foods do you **shun**? Why?

5. Which rooms in your house are likely to smell **musty**? Explain.

6. What would you do if there were a **stench** in your room? Why?

7. When might an actor **deviate** from the script? Explain.

8. What **prerogatives** do you have that a young child does not have? Explain.

9. What is something you might have to **unfetter** yourself from? Explain.

10. What does mold need to **flourish** in? Explain.

VOCABULARY

harness When you harness something, you take control of it and direct how it is used.

waver When someone or something wavers, it moves back and forth or cannot make a decision.

eternal Something that is eternal has no beginning and no end.

shun If you shun something, you stay away from it because you don't want to be involved with it.

musty Something that is musty smells damp and old.

stench If something has a stench, it has a very terrible smell.

deviate If you deviate from something, you go a different direction or do things differently than was planned.

prerogative If you say that something is your prerogative, you claim the right or privilege to do it.

unfetter When you unfetter something, you free it.

flourish If something flourishes, it is healthy, strong, and successful.

Take It Further

Complete these sentences on a separate piece of paper.

1. A scientist might **harness** the power of electricity to . . .

2. Devon **wavered** before agreeing to go to the movie because . . .

3. The math test felt **eternal** because . . .

4. Haley thought her brother was **shunning** her because he . . .

5. My favorite T-shirt had a **musty** smell after I . . .

6. The **stench** in Ms. Katella's room was caused by . . .

7. Violet **deviated** from her usual route home when . . .

8. Jermaine felt it was his **prerogative** to . . .

9. Will felt **unfettered** when he . . .

10. In order to **flourish** as a dancer, I need . . .

Explore It

You know the word *eternal* by now, but are you familiar with two of its most common synonyms, *permanent* and *interminable*?

permanent
If something is permanent, it cannot be changed.

interminable
Something that is interminable is boring and seems to last forever.

> Working with someone else, complete the following sentences. Each word has a slightly different meaning, so remember to change the end of each sentence depending on the word used. Be prepared to explain your group's work.

1. Marta thought the story was eternal because . . .

2. Marta thought the story was permanent because . . .

3. Marta thought the story was interminable because . . .

For Your EARS Only

Ever talk so fast that adults couldn't keep up? If they blamed their aging ears, they weren't wrong. The adults around you may be better than you at some things, but you are probably better at hearing!

In fact, you can hear some high-pitched noises that most adults can't. Sounds quite useful, doesn't it? Actually, the first people who harnessed it used it against teens. Business owners in Wales felt it was their prerogative to begin using alarms that were painful to teenagers' ears. The alarms would keep teenagers from hanging around the shopping centers. But most adults couldn't hear the alarms. If they could, they didn't sound as loud and annoying. The adults could shop unfettered while the teens were driven away.

Now, the same discovery is being used by teens. Some new ring tones make sounds so high-pitched that most adults can't hear them. Now, your social life can flourish anywhere you want it to. Your phone can tell you that you have a text message. It just won't annoy most adults!

97

After Dark

Hercules, the great horned owl of Pfishinger Pass, sat silently on the tree branch and watched the young boy stumble his way through the dark forest. He blinked his human-sized eyes at the boy's clumsiness, wondering why the human had not seen the vine sticking up from the ground before him. Humans were eternally foolish when wandering through the woods after dark.

Eric knew he was out too late, but he was fascinated by the great horned owl that lived in the forest behind his family's house. He was amazed that they could swivel their heads in almost a complete circle and hear sounds that were ten times fainter than anything humans could hear, but they could hardly smell anything at all. He was determined to get a look at the great bird, and he figured night was his best chance.

Hercules watched the boy's progress with one eye; meanwhile, he had heard a soft rustling in the leaves just beyond where the boy was struggling to see in the dark. He focused on the area with his other eye and spotted a small brown mouse. Without hesitating, Hercules spread his wings and swooped silently down on the mouse, grabbed it in his sharp talons and soared back up into a tree.

Eric was working to unfetter himself from a bush when he felt something move past him in the darkness. It was huge—it had a wingspan of almost five feet! He heard it snatch something, and then it was gone, as silently as it had come. His heart was pounding, and he knew he had just been as close as he ever would be to a great horned owl.

Rev Up Your Writing

A better sense of hearing can have its advantages. Make a list of some advantages and disadvantages of having better hearing. Use your list to write about the benefits and drawbacks. Use as many of the vocabulary words as possible but make sense.

Word Organizer

Copy this graphic organizer onto a separate piece of paper.

List words that are synonyms of *stench*. Write your answers in the Synonyms box. Use some of the words in this box to describe a food that you think smells awful.

Then list words that are antonyms of *stench*. Write your answers in the Antonyms box. Use some of the words in this box to describe a food that you think smells pleasant.

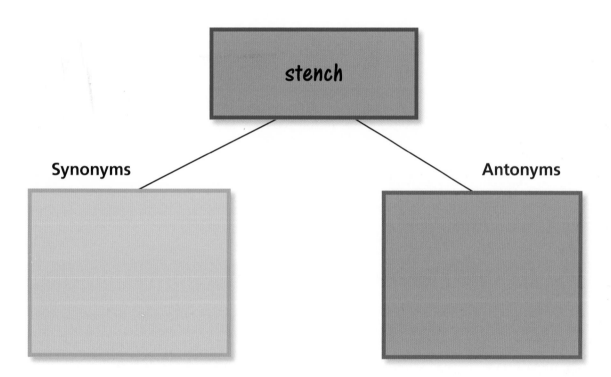

stench

Synonyms

Antonyms

The Nose Knows, But Do YOU?

Stench Warfare

Some governments are looking into non-deadly military techniques. One such technique involves using super stink bombs to disperse mobs and keep people away from restricted areas. As the horrible odor spreads through the area, people first waver, unsure of what they smell. As the stench becomes worse, the part of the brain that controls emotions is triggered and the brain labels the unknown smell as dangerous, causing people to run in terror for safety.

A Smelly Solution

London debt collector Andy Smulion uses a unique technique: he simply shows up at the debtor's place of business smelling like a horrific mixture of skunk, sewage, and raw eggs. He stays at their office until they can stand the stench no longer, at which point they pay him the money they owe and promptly shun him. It's a great job for Andy, who has permanently blocked sinuses.

Long-Distance Smellers

An elephant's trunk can smell water up to three miles away, and a male luna moth can smell a female as far away as five miles.

Dog-Gone-It, That's a Sensitive Schnoz!

If you're tracking something with a bloodhound and the dog wants to deviate from your path, you should probably follow it. Bloodhounds can follow scents that are nearly four days old, and the part of a nose that detects smells is 50 times bigger in a bloodhound than in a human. And sheepdogs can smell 44 times better than humans!

It's All in How You Smell It

Smells are not always good or bad. Research shows that people get used to smells in much the same way they get used to certain foods. People who grow up on ranches often like the musty smell of nature and horse manure, and some people even like the smell of skunks!

One-Track Nose

A male silkworm can smell a potential mate up to seven miles away but can smell nothing else.

Rev Up Your Writing

Smells can have strong effects on people. Write about a smell that has a strong effect on you. What does it make you think of? How does it make you feel? Use as many of the vocabulary words as possible but make sense.

101

Can You Relate?

Copy this graphic organizer onto a separate piece of paper. Match the following words with their related vocabulary word. If a word relates to more than one vocabulary word, explain why.

alienate   If you alienate people, you cause them to feel like they don't belong.

contempt   When you feel contempt for someone or something, your opinion of it is very low.

extricate   If you extricate someone, you get him or her out of a difficult situation.

misanthrope   A misanthrope is a person who does not like others.

wayward   People who are wayward are unpredictable and have their own way of doing things.

deviate	shun	unfetter

In Your Own Words

Respond to one of the following prompts on a separate piece of paper. As you respond, use as many of the vocabulary words as possible. Be creative but make sense!

▶ Write about a time when you or a friend decided to make your own decisions and not follow the crowd. Why did you make that choice? What did you learn from the experience?

▶ Write a short story from an animal's point of view. Describe how it feels and how people treat it. Explain how its senses are different and what special abilities it has.

▶ Write about a topic of your choice.

VOCABULARY

harness
waver
eternal
shun
musty
stench
deviate
prerogative
unfetter
flourish

THE STORY OF
ARACHNE

Retold by Kelly Daigle
Illustrated by Olwyn Whelan

In ancient Greece, a young woman named Arachne declares herself the best weaver in the world. But when she boasts that she weaves even better than the goddess Athena, the townspeople know that she's asking for trouble.

There once lived in Greece a maiden named Arachne. Even though she lived in a small village, a village she had never left, she was known throughout the land. She was not famous because she was young and pretty, but because she was extraordinarily skilled on the weaving loom.[1] Arachne's exquisitely embroidered cloths were the finest anyone had ever seen. People came from far and wide to watch Arachne work and to buy her beautiful tapestries.[2]

Arachne was skilled, but she was conceited as well. She would brag loudly about her talent to anyone who was near and willing to listen. As time went on, her boasts grew larger and larger. She went from saying she was the best weaver in Greece to claiming to be the best weaver in the world. Then, she declared rashly one day that her skill topped[3] even that of Athena, the goddess of, among other things, arts and crafts.

When the people heard her say this, they grew nervous and warned her that she should not incur the wrath of the gods by claiming to be better than them.

"Why not?" Arachne demanded insolently. "I am better than Athena. If she wants to prove her skill, let her come down here and compete with me."

Day after day Arachne repeated her rash claim that she was more skilled at weaving than even Athena herself, and day after day called for Athena to come and compete with her so that the matter could be decided once and for all.

Finally, Athena grew so annoyed that she could no longer ignore Arachne's arrogance. She traveled to Arachne's cottage one day in the guise of an old beggar woman and stood in the crowd that had gathered to watch Arachne work. Before long, Arachne began bragging about her skill, and once again she declared herself to be more talented than even the goddess Athena.

Athena, still disguised as the old beggar woman, spoke up.

"Child," Athena began, "you are still young. You have great talent, but you lack the years that would have given you wisdom. It is not wise to speak so brazenly against the gods. You should thank them for the gift of weaving they have given you rather than tempting their anger."

FOOTNOTES
1 *loom:* frame used for weaving thread or yarn into cloth
2 *tapestries:* artwork made by weaving cloth
3 *topped:* was better than

Arachne was indignant[4] that an old beggar woman would speak to her in such a manner.

"Old woman!" she cried. "What do you know of gifts? If you had any talent at all when you were younger, you would not have ended up so poor. Do not lecture me about something you know nothing about."

Incensed at Arachne's response, Athena shed her guise as the old woman and stood before the crowd in robes of dazzling silver and white. Her eyes flashed at Arachne, and the crowd fell to the floor, terrified to be in the presence of a goddess.

"I know nothing of talent?" Athena asked Arachne in a voice cold with anger. "It was I who gave you your gift of weaving. Now let's see what you can do with it." Athena motioned for two new looms to be brought.

Arachne had never meant to actually compete with Athena, but she saw the crowd around her and knew that she could never back down[5] after all her boasting and bragging.

"Yes," Arachne said obstinately. "Let's see what I can do."

Both women set to work immediately, and the crowd of onlookers pressed in[6] closer than ever before. None of them had ever witnessed a competition between a mortal and a goddess before. Both Arachne and Athena were skilled beyond belief. Their fingers flew deftly[7] through the strings, creating beautiful scenes in just seconds. Athena was creating a picture of her birth, during which she sprang from the head of Zeus, her father, fully grown and armed for battle. Around the edges of her piece were the other gods and goddesses, each busy doing what they enjoyed most: Apollo playing music, Artemis hunting, Dionysus enjoying a feast, and so on. Arachne was creating a pastoral scene of fields and flowers. In it, she was holding a cloth she had created and there were figures at her feet, worshipping her and her skill.

As the two women drew closer to finishing their pieces, the crowd could clearly see that, even though it was Arachne's finest work ever, Athena's tapestry was clearly better.

A murmur began to spread through the crowd as they realized that Arachne had been beaten. She heard the rising noise and the hair on the back of her neck and her arms began to stand on end. She realized what had happened before she even stepped back to examine the two cloths.

FOOTNOTES
4 *indignant:* angry about something that seems unfair
5 *back down:* give up
6 *pressed in:* came close
7 *deftly:* with skill

Ashamed of her defeat, Arachne could not bear to face Athena or the crowd. She quickly grabbed a rope and ran to a chair, attempting to hang herself to escape from her shame.

"You fool," Athena said as she watched Arachne tie the knot in the rope and slip it over her head. "Even now you will not repent your folly.[8] Since you show no remorse for what you have done, I will condemn you to a life of endless weaving."

With that, Athena transformed[9] Arachne into a tiny spider and the rope into the spider's thread.

"You were so proud of your weaving. Now you and your descendents will do nothing but weave, day in and day out, for eternity."[10]

FOOTNOTES
....
8 *repent your folly:* admit you were wrong
9 *transformed:* changed
10 *for eternity:* forever

Explain Yourself

Answer each question on a separate piece of paper. Be sure to explain your answers.

1. Would you fly in an airplane with a pilot who behaves **rashly**? Why or why not?

2. What would you **incur** if you went to the movies without permission? Explain.

3. What would you do if your brother or sister were **insolent** to you?

4. If you could wear any **guise**, what would you wear? Why?

5. What is one thing that **incenses** you? Explain.

6. How would you deal with an **obstinate** friend?

7. Would you forgive a friend if she told you she felt **remorse**? Explain.

8. Would you **condemn** your dog for barking? Why or why not?

9. At what activity do you think you are most **adept**? Why?

10. Would winning the election for class president make someone **arrogant**? Why or why not?

VOCABULARY

rashly If you act rashly, you act too quickly and without thinking.

incur When you incur something unpleasant, it happens because of something you did.

insolent An insolent person is rude and disrespectful.

guise A guise is a false appearance.

incensed If you are incensed about something, you are extremely angry and insulted by it.

obstinate If you are obstinate, you are stubborn.

remorse If you feel remorse about something you did, you feel guilt and regret.

condemn If someone is condemned, he or she is thought to be guilty and is punished.

adept Someone who is adept is very good at doing something.

arrogant Arrogant people think they are better than everyone else.

Take It Further

Complete these sentences on a separate piece of paper.

1. Because Zach had spoken too **rashly** in his discussion with the principal, he . . .

2. When Jason stepped on the president's foot, he **incurred** . . .

3. "You are so **insolent**!" my mother said to me, after I . . .

4. Karina puts on a **guise** when she . . .

5. I was **incensed** when my best friend . . .

6. During the jumping contest, Kayla's horse **obstinately** . . .

7. Ryan felt **remorseful** after eating the pizza his brother had saved, so he . . .

8. The man was **condemned** to walk . . .

9. We realized that the juggler was not **adept** when . . .

10. "How **arrogant**," said Jasmine. "Did you see how that guy . . .?

Explore It

By now, you know the word *incur*. But do you know where it came from? It actually goes all the way back to a Latin word *incurrere*, which comes from the prefix *in–*, which means "toward," and *currere*, which means "run." So, when you incur something—like somebody's anger— you're actually running toward it!

Work in a group to create a funny story about someone who is "running toward" his or her own doom. Be sure to use the word *incur* at least once. Be prepared to share your story with the rest of the class!

Rescue!

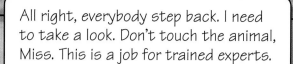

All right, everybody step back. I need to take a look. Don't touch the animal, Miss. This is a job for trained experts.

Who does she think she is?

Don't be insolent. She's the ranger.

You want some help? Or should we still stay away?

Help! Please!

You are remarkably adept in a crisis. Most people panic when they see a stranded animal.

Thanks! Keya, I think that was enough excitement.

Me, too!

A Dolphin's Sleep Guise

Because of their undersea environment, mammals like the dolphin have to be conscious to breathe. This means they have to sleep with one eye open and rest their brain at the same time. This allows them to protect themselves from predators and rise to the surface to breathe.

Rev Up Your Writing

The graphic novel shows an unusual encounter between people and an animal. Have you or someone you know ever had a strange or amazing animal encounter? Write about what happened. Use as may of the vocabulary words as possible but make sense.

Word Organizer

Copy this graphic organizer onto a separate piece of paper.

List things a cat might be adept at and write your answers under the cat column. Then list things a monkey might be adept at and write your answers under the monkey column. Explain your answers.

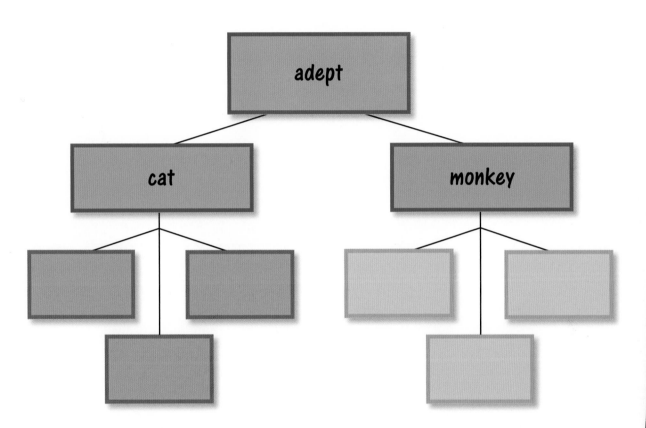

Famous & Furry

Q: . . . And in this episode of *Movie Madness,* we have Carly Hsu, a trainer who works with the Hollywood canines, or dogs, in our favorite movies. So, Carly, our viewers want to know—Where do you get your canine stars?

CH: About four out of five acting dogs originally came from animal shelters. If we hadn't found them, they would probably have been condemned to a life in a cage. Our trainers adopt them and become their loving owners.

Q: It's fantastic that you can help them like that. How do you decide which dog to take?

CH: We look for dogs with personality, dogs that are yapping in their cages. We also look for happy, obedient dogs we can train easily. Personally, I'm remorseful that we can't take them all. But, we try our best to work with as many shelter animals as we can.

Q: What if a dog is too obstinate to follow directions?

CH: Obstinate dogs don't last long in this business. We do make sure we give them tasks that they do well, though. For example, we used three dogs in one role for our last movie. One was great at jumping, another was good at running, and the third—well, he just lay around. But, he was really good at it!

Q: How did you pick three dogs that looked exactly the same?

CH: We didn't. We chose a star, one that would do most of the work. Then, we dyed and trimmed the fur of three similar dogs. This made them look identical to the first dog. My dogs even have their own hair and makeup artists!

INCREDIBLE! Thanks, Carly. Tune in next week, to Movie Madness—the talk show about the movies you love!

Ask Ms. Pooch

Dear Ms. Pooch:
My dog has a lot of personality. I think he could be great on TV or in the movies. How can I help him become a star?

Signed,
Doggone Curious in Denver

Dear Doggone,
Ah, doggie stardom! It's a dream that all pups have, but only a select few get to experience (including yours truly, the fabulous Ms. Pooch).

To make your dog's dream come true, be ready to incur some hefty bills. Beauty costs, my dear, and you can't make it in Hollywood if you are scruffy. The Benji look is out, way out. Glam, glam, glam, is in! Go to the finest groomers. Make sure all that loose fur is history. Make those teeth pearly white and sparkling.

Next, get professional photos taken. A good photographer will know what the studios are looking for, so when he says, "Jump," ask him how high!

Manners are a good thing. Nobody likes an arrogant co-star. Obedience is also important. Your dog must go beyond the basics of "sit" and "stay." He needs to be able to respond to cues flawlessly, take after take. Many can't handle the pressure and leave Tinseltown with their tails between their legs. But if you're willing to take the big leap, I say go for it. Work hard and earn a star on the walk of fame. That'll be something to bark about!

See you in the movies,

Ms. Pooch

Rev Up Your Writing

Both interviews and letters are great ways to communicate. Make up an interview with someone whose work or life you know about or write a letter to a friend describing something interesting that has happened to you. Use as many of the vocabulary words as possible but make sense.

Can You Relate?

Copy this graphic organizer onto a separate piece of paper. Match the following words with their related vocabulary word. If a word relates to more than one vocabulary word, explain why.

boor   A boor is a person who is crude and unrefined.
impudent   If someone is impudent, he acts rudely or disrespectfully.
irascible   An irascible person gets mad easily.
livid   A person described as livid is extremely angry.
provocative   Something that is provocative tends to make people angry.

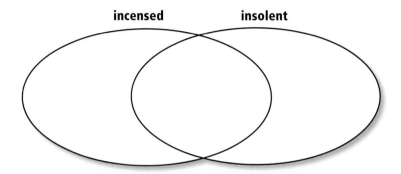

incensed   insolent

In Your Own Words

VOCABULARY

rashly
incur
insolent
guise
incensed
obstinate
remorse
condemn
adept
arrogant

Respond to one of the following prompts on a separate piece of paper. As you respond, use as many of the vocabulary words as possible. Be creative but make sense!

▶ Write about a time when you or someone you know had to react very quickly to a situation, as Jada and Keya did when they found the dolphin. What happened? How did things turn out?

▶ Write a short story from the point of view of a pet. Have your narrator describe its owners and the other animals in the neighborhood. Have the pet go on an adventure!

▶ Write about a topic of your choice.

Sleeping with the Meerkats

By Yann Martel
Illustrated by Winson Trang

A young man stranded in a lifeboat with a 450-pound Bengal tiger named Richard Parker washes up on the banks of a floating island. What mysteries will he find there?

Eventually I quit the boat.[1] It seemed absurd to spend my nights in such cramped quarters[2] with an animal who was becoming roomy in his needs,[3] when I could have an entire island. I decided the safe thing to do would be to sleep in a tree. Richard Parker's nocturnal[4] practice of sleeping in the lifeboat was never a law in my mind. It would not be a good idea for me to be outside my territory, sleeping and defenseless on the ground, the one time he decided to go for a midnight stroll.

So one day I left the boat with the net, a rope and some blankets. I sought out a handsome tree on the edge of the forest and threw the rope over the lowest branch. My fitness was such[5] that I had no problem pulling myself up by my arms and climbing the tree. I found two solid branches that were level and close together, and I tied the net to them. I returned at the end of the day.

I had just finished folding the blankets to make my mattress when I detected a commotion among the meerkats. I looked. I pushed aside branches to see better. I looked in every direction and as far as the horizon. It was unmistakable. The meerkats were abandoning the ponds—indeed, the whole plain—and rapidly making for the forest.[6] An entire nation of meerkats was on the move, their backs arched and their feet a blur. I was wondering what further surprise these animals held in store[7] for me when I noticed with consternation that the ones from the pond closest to me had surrounded my tree and were climbing up the trunk. The trunk was disappearing under a wave of determined meerkats. I thought they were coming to attack me, that here was the reason why Richard Parker slept in the lifeboat: during the day the meerkats were docile and harmless, but at night, under their collective weight, they crushed their enemies ruthlessly. I was both afraid and indignant. To survive for so long in a lifeboat with a 450-pound Bengal tiger only to die up a tree at the hands of two-pound meerkats struck me as a tragedy too unfair and too ridiculous to bear.[8]

FOOTNOTES

[1] *quit the boat:* stopped sleeping in the boat
[2] *cramped quarters:* small living space
[3] *roomy in his needs:* needs a lot of living space
[4] *nocturnal:* nighttime
[5] *my fitness was such..:* my health was good enough that...
[6] *making for the forest:* going toward the forest
[7] *held in store:* had waiting
[8] *to bear:* to allow or accept

They meant me no harm. They climbed up to me, over me, about me—and past me. They settled upon every branch in the tree. It became *laden* with them. They even took over my bed. And the same as far as the eye could see. They were climbing every tree in sight. The entire forest was turning brown, an autumn that came in a few minutes. Collectively, as they scampered by in droves[9] to claim empty trees deeper into the forest, they made more noise than a stampeding herd of elephants.

The plain, meanwhile, was becoming bare and depopulated.

From a bunk bed with a tiger to an overcrowded dormitory[10] with meerkats—will I be believed when I say that life can take the most surprising turns? I jostled[11] with meerkats so that I could have a place in my own bed. They snuggled up to me. Not a square inch of space was left free.

They settled down and stopped squeaking and chirping. Silence came to the tree. We fell asleep.

I woke up at dawn covered from head to toe in a living fur blanket. Some meerkittens had discovered the warmer parts of my body. I had a tight, sweaty collar of them around my neck—and it must have been their mother who had settled herself so contentedly on the side of my head . . .

They left the tree as briskly and as unceremoniously as they had invaded it. It was the same with every tree around. The plain grew thick with meerkats, and the noises of their day started filling the air. The tree looked empty. And I felt empty, a little. I had liked the experience of sleeping with the meerkats.

I began to sleep in the tree every night. I emptied the lifeboat of useful items and made myself a nice treetop bedroom. I got used to the unintentional scratches I received from meerkats climbing over me. My only complaint would be that animals higher up occasionally relieved themselves on me.

One night the meerkats woke me up. They were chattering and shaking. I sat up and looked in the direction they were looking. The sky was cloudless and the moon full. The land was robbed of its color. Everything glowed strangely in shades of black, grey and white. It was the pond. Silver shapes were moving in it, emerging from below and breaking the black surface of the water.

Fish. Dead fish. They were floating up from deep down. The pond—remember, forty feet across—was filling up with all kinds of dead fish until its surface was no longer black but silver. And from the way the surface kept on being disturbed, it was evident that more dead fish were coming up.

FOOTNOTES
9 *droves:* in large numbers, like a herd
10 *dormitory:* a room or building that provides sleeping areas for many people
11 *jostled:* pushed, wrestled

By the time a dead shark quietly appeared, the meerkats were in a fury of excitement, shrieking like tropical birds. The hysteria spread to the neighboring trees. It was deafening. I wondered whether I was about to see the sight of fish being hauled up trees.

Not a single meerkat went down to the pond. None even made the first motions of going down. They did no more than loudly express their frustration.

I found the sight sinister. There was something disturbing about all those dead fish.

I lay down again and fought to go back to sleep over the meerkats' racket. At first light I was stirred from my slumber by the hullabaloo they made trooping[12] down the tree. Yawning and stretching, I looked down at the pond that had been the source of such fire and fluster[13] the previous night.

It was empty. Or nearly. But it wasn't the work of the meerkats. They were just now diving in to get what was left.

The fish had disappeared. I was confounded. Was I looking at the wrong pond? No, for sure it was that one. Was I certain it was not the meerkats that had emptied it? Absolutely. I could hardly see them heaving an entire shark out of water, let alone carrying it on their backs and disappearing with it. Could it be Richard Parker? Possibly in part, but not an entire pond in one night.

It was a complete mystery. No amount of staring into the pond and at its deep green walls could explain to me what had happened to the fish. The next night I looked, but no new fish came into the pond.

The answer to the mystery came sometime later, from deep within the forest.

FOOTNOTES

[12] *hullabaloo they made trooping:* the loud noise they made while they marched

[13] *the source of such fire and fluster:* the cause of so much excitement and confusion

Explain Yourself

VOCABULARY

Answer each question on a separate piece of paper. Be sure to explain your answers.

1. Would seeing a mysterious stranger outside your door make you feel **consternation**? Why or why not?

2. Would you take a **docile** dog for a walk around small children? Why or why not?

3. Would you become **indignant** if you had to take a cooking and sewing class? Why or why not?

4. Which is more heavily **laden**, an ant carrying breadcrumbs or an elephant carrying five people? Explain.

5. What might you say to a friend who eats **unceremoniously** during a meal with your family?

6. If you hear a **sinister** laugh from behind a door, would you open the door? Why or why not?

7. What **confounds** you about people of the opposite gender? Explain.

8. Should a **boisterous** group of people be allowed into a library? Why or why not?

9. What do you do when faced with a **conundrum** during a test? Explain.

10. If people are leaving a movie theater with **unsettled** looks on their faces, would you want to see the movie? Why or why not?

consternation   Consternation is a feeling of nervousness or alarm.

docile   Someone or something that is docile is calm and easy to control.

indignant   If you are indignant, you are angry about something that seems unfair.

laden   If someone or something is laden, it is carrying heavy things or burdens.

unceremoniously   If you do something unceremoniously, you do it quickly and without manners.

sinister   Something sinister is evil looking and scary.

confound   If something confounds you, it confuses you.

boisterous   Someone or something that is boisterous is noisy and excited.

conundrum   A conundrum is a mystery, puzzle, or problem.

unsettling   Something unsettling makes you feel uneasy or disturbed.

119

Take It Further

Complete these sentences on a separate piece of paper.

1. The bus driver was filled with **consternation** when . . .

2. A **docile** tiger is likely to . . .

3. Kelly became **indignant** after Mr. Martin told her to . . .

4. When Nanette saw her grandma **laden** with shopping bags, she . . .

5. Marcia **unceremoniously** invited me to her slumber party after . . .

6. Jorge's brother gave him a **sinister** look when . . .

7. I was **confounded** when my neighbor . . .

8. Tim and LaTisha are usually very **boisterous** when . . .

9. Mr. Lucas likes to start the class with a **conundrum** because . . .

10. My science teacher had an **unsettling** feeling after . . .

Explore It

Over time, the original meaning of a word can affect the meaning of related words. For example, the word *sinister* **was Latin for "left" or "unlucky." Now** *sinister* **means "evil." The idea of being "unlucky" or "not right" has also been attached to the word** *left***.**

Discuss the meaning of the following phrases with your group. Try to provide an explanation for each sentence. Be prepared to share your findings with the class.

two left feet:
Hala dances with two left feet. She keeps tripping over her own dress.

out in left field:
Shawn's answer to this simple question was way out in left field. I wondered if he really read the assignment last night.

left-handed compliment:
"Cheryl, those are really nice earrings. Did you find them in a garbage can?"

OPTICAL ILLUSIONS
Explained

LOOK AT THIS PICTURE

WARNING!
If you suddenly feel dizzy or unsettled, look away from the page. Some people cannot take the mental overload!

MORE
ILLUSIONS EXPLAINED ON NEXT PAGE

See the Old Woman?

(Confounded? Here's a hint: the young woman's chin is the old woman's nose!)

This picture is an example of a visual or optical illusion. An optical illusion is something that plays tricks on your visual system. When you look at something, your eyes send a message to your brain. In your brain, the message is matched to images already stored in your memory. When you looked at the picture of the women, your brain would not let you see both images at the same time. Your eyes had to send a different set of messages to your brain for you to see the old woman.

Did You Know?

A psychologist named Hermann Rorshach developed a special test that used inkblots similar to this one. To conduct the test, Rorshach would show patients inkblots and ask them to describe what they saw. Based on their answers, Rorshach was able to tell if they were laden with stress or consternation about something. Some patients may have reported seeing a sinister looking face on some cards while others may have reported seeing animals.

Rev Up Your Writing

Write about a time when you or someone you know was tricked by a picture or something else you "thought" you saw. Use as many vocabulary words as possible but make sense.

Word Organizer

Copy this graphic organizer onto a separate piece of paper.

List events that you would find unsettling in the top half of the Word Wheel.
List events that are not unsettling in the bottom half.

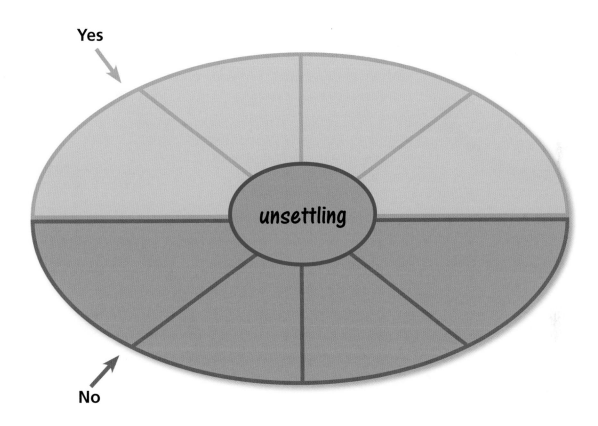

Yes

unsettling

No

Ask a BRAINIAC!

Dr. Neuro

Dear Dr. Neuro,

I know people think and learn in different ways. I was wondering why I'm a whiz at some things, but weak in others. For example, I can program a computer game and solve complex math problems in seconds, but I get completely confused and frustrated if I have to draw a picture or write a poem. Why is that?

—Curious in California

Dear Curious in California,

The answer to this conundrum lies in how you use your brain. Some people claim that we rely on either the left or right sides of our brains. This theory claims that the right side of the brain deals with creative concepts while the left side of the brain deals with logic.

If this theory is correct, a person who prefers to use the right side of his brain might learn better working in groups, using pictures, or creating art. This person might become indignant if you don't allow him to be imaginative. According to the theory, you are the type of person who prefers using the left part of your brain. You might enjoy working through problems by yourself rather than in a group. A "left-brained" person might complain unceremoniously just to avoid sitting through a pottery class.

Obviously, these are very general ideas of how people think. In reality, you use all of your brain. However, if you believe the theory, you might want to pick some creative activities to exercise your brain a bit.

Regards,

Dr. Neuro

Which side of your brain do you use the most?

Do you believe this theory? Read the following questions to see if the theory works for you.

	A	**B**
If I had a choice between dog walking and baby-sitting, I would choose —	dog walking; dogs are more docile than children.	baby-sitting; children are more fun to play with and entertain.
If I had to fix my mother's high-heeled shoe, I would —	look in the telephone directory for a shoe repair company.	grab the really strong glue or a hammer and nail.
During my free time, I might choose to —	play chess so I can develop my strategy.	create a mosaic using things I find around the house.
When I am with my friends, I —	like to play trivia games.	like to do boisterous things like skateboarding.

If you answered **A** to most of these questions, you like to use the left side of your brain more.

If you answered **B** to most of these questions, you prefer using the right side of your brain.

In either case, always remember that you are really using both sides of your brain (to some degree) when completing any task!

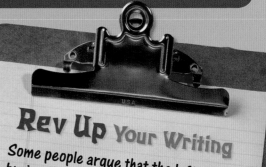

Rev Up Your Writing

Some people argue that the left-brained and right-brained idea is false and that people just have different ways of doing things. What is your opinion of the theory? Do you think your favorite activities give clues about how your brain works? Use as many vocabulary words as possible but make sense.

Can You Relate?

Copy this graphic organizer onto a separate piece of paper. Match the following words with their related vocabulary word. If a word relates to more than one word, explain why.

enigmatic   Enigmatic things are puzzling, mysterious, or hard to understand.
lurid   If something is lurid, it causes horror, fear, or shock.
onerous   If a task is onerous, it is difficult and hard to carry out.
pariah   If someone is a pariah, he or she is an outcast from society.
querulous   A querulous person complains about things a lot.

laden	consternation	conundrum

In Your Own Words

Respond to one of the following prompts on a separate piece of paper. As you respond, use as many of the vocabulary words as possible. Be creative but make sense!

► Write about a time when you or someone you know saw something that you couldn't explain. Did it scare you? Why or why not? What did you do? Did you ever figure out a logical explanation for it?

► Some people say that humans only use 10% of their brains. If you were Dr. Neuro, what would you say to the people who believe this? Take a position and convince others that you are right.

► Write about a topic of your choice.

VOCABULARY

consternation
docile
indignant
laden
unceremoniously
sinister
confound
boisterous
conundrum
unsettling

The Living Kuan-yin

Retold by Carol Kendall
and Yao-Wen Li
Illustrated by Twila Schofield

*Chin Po-wan is rich. His last name
even means "gold." So when Po-wan
runs out of money, he goes on a journey
to find out why. Will Po-wan find
the answers he seeks, or will
his desire to help others
get in his way?*

Even though the family name of Chin means "gold," it does not signify that everyone of that name is rich. Long ago, in the province of Chekiang, however, there was a certain wealthy Chin family of whom it was popularly said that its fortune was as great as its name. It seemed quite fitting, then, when a son was born to the family, that he should be called Po-wan, "Million," for he was certain to be worth a million pieces of gold when he came of age.

With such a happy circumstance of names, Po-wan himself never doubted that he would have a never-ending supply of money . . . and he spent it accordingly—not on himself, but on any unfortunate who came to his attention. He had a deep sense of compassion for anyone in distress of body or spirit: a poor man had only to hold out his hand, and Po-wan poured gold into it; if a destitute widow and her brood of starvelings[1] but lifted sorrowful eyes to his, he provided them with food and lodging and friendship for the rest of their days.

In such ways did he live that even a million gold pieces were not enough to support him. His resources so dwindled that finally he scarcely had enough food for himself, his clothes flapped threadbare[2] on his wasted frame, and the cold seeped into his bone marrow for lack of a fire. Still he gave away the little money that came to him.

One day, as he scraped out half of his bowl of rice for a beggar even hungrier than he, he began to ponder on his destitute state.

"Why am I so poor?" he wondered. "I have never spent extravagantly. I have never, from the day of my birth, done an evil deed. Why, then, am I, whose very name is A Million Pieces of Gold, no longer able to find even a copper to give this unfortunate creature, and have only a bowl of rice to share with him?"

He thought long about his situation and at last determined to go without delay to the South Sea. Therein, it was told, dwelt the all-merciful goddess, the Living Kuan-yin, who could tell the past and future. He would put his question to her, and she would tell him the answer.

Soon he had left his home country behind and traveled for many weeks in unfamiliar lands. One day he found his way barred by a wide and furiously flowing river. As he stood first on one foot and then on the other, wondering how he could possibly get across, he heard a commanding voice calling from the top of an overhanging cliff.

FOOTNOTES
1 *brood of starvelings:* starving children
2 *threadbare:* thin, worn out fabric

"Chin Po-wan!" the voice said. "If you are going to the South Sea, please ask the Living Kuan-yin a question for me!"

"Yes, yes, of course," Po-wan agreed at once, for he had never in his life refused a request made of him. In any case, the Living Kuan-yin permitted each person who approached her three questions, and he had but one of his own to ask.

Craning his head towards the voice coming from above, he suddenly began to tremble, for the speaker was a gigantic snake with a body as large as a temple column. Po-wan was glad he had agreed so readily to the request.

"Ask her, then," said the snake, "why I am not yet a dragon, even though I have practiced self-denial for more than one thousand years."

"That I will do, and gl-gladly," stammered Po-wan, hoping that the snake would continue to practice self-denial just a bit longer. "But, your . . . your Snakery . . . or your Serpentry, perhaps I should say . . . that is . . . you see, don't you . . . first I must cross this raging river, and I know not how."

"That is no problem at all," said the snake. "I shall carry you across, of course."

"Of course," Po-wan echoed weakly. Overcoming his fear and his reluctance to touch the slippery-slithery scales, Chin Po-wan climbed onto the snake's back and rode across quite safely. Politely, and just a bit hurriedly, he thanked the self-denying serpent and bade him good-bye. Then he continued on his way to the South Sea.

By noon he was very hungry. Fortunately, a nearby inn offered meals at a price he could afford. While waiting for his bowl of rice, he chatted with the innkeeper and told him of the Snake of the Cliff, which the innkeeper knew well and respected, for the serpent always denied bandits the crossing of the river. Inadvertently, during the exchange of stories, Po-wan revealed the purpose of his journey.

"Why, then," cried the innkeeper, "let me prevail upon your generosity to ask a word for me." He laid an appealing hand on Po-wan's ragged sleeve. "I have a beautiful daughter," he said, "wonderfully amiable[3] and pleasing of disposition. But although she is in her twentieth year, she has never in all her life uttered a single word. I should be very much obliged if you would ask the Living Kuan-yin why she is unable to speak."

Po-wan, much moved by the innkeeper's plea for his mute daughter, of course promised to do so. For after all, the Living Kuan-yin allowed each person three questions, and he had but one of his own to ask.

FOOTNOTES
. . . .
3 *amiable:* friendly

Nightfall found him far from any inn, but there were houses in the neighborhood, and he asked for lodging at the largest. The owner, a man obviously of great wealth, was pleased to offer him a bed in a fine chamber but first begged him to partake of a hot meal and good drink. Po-wan ate well, slept soundly, and, much refreshed, was about to depart the following morning when his good host, having learned that Po-wan was journeying to the South Sea, asked if he would be kind enough to put a question for him to the Living Kuan-yin.

"For twenty years," he said, "from the time this house was built, my garden has been cultivated with the utmost care; yet in all those years, not one tree, not one small plant, has bloomed or borne[4] fruit, and because of this, no bird comes to sing, nor bee to gather nectar. I don't like to put you to a bother, Chin Po-wan, but as you are going to the South Sea anyway, perhaps you would not mind seeking out the Living Kuan-yin and asking her why the plants in my garden don't bloom."

"I shall be delighted to put the question to her," said Po-wan. For after all, the Living Kuan-yin allowed each person three questions, and he had but . . .

Traveling onward, Po-wan examined the quandary[5] in which he found himself. The Living Kuan-yin allowed but three questions, and he had somehow, without quite knowing how, accumulated four questions. One of them would have to go unasked, but which? If he left out his own question, his whole journey would have been in vain. If, on the other hand, he left out the question of the snake, or the innkeeper, or the kind host, he would break his promise and betray their faith in him.

"A promise should never be made if it cannot be kept," he told himself. "I made the promises and therefore I must keep them. Besides, the journey will not be in vain, for at least some of these problems will be solved by the Living Kuan-yin. Furthermore, assisting others must certainly be counted as a good deed, and the more good deeds abroad in the land, the better for everyone, including me."

At last he came into the presence of the Living Kuan-yin.

First he asked the serpent's question: "Why is the Snake of the Cliff not yet a dragon, although he has practiced self-denial for more than one thousand years?"

FOOTNOTES
4 *borne:* produced
5 *quandary:* problem

And the Living Kuan-yin answered: "On his head are seven bright pearls. If he removes six of them, he can become a dragon."

Next, Po-wan asked the innkeeper's question: "Why is the innkeeper's daughter unable to speak, although she is in the twentieth year of her life?"

And the Living Kuan-yin answered: "It is her fate to remain mute until she sees the man destined to be her husband."

Last, Po-wan asked the kind host's question: "Why are there never blossoms in the rich man's garden, although it has been carefully cultivated for twenty years?"

And the Living Kuan-yin answered: "Buried in the garden are seven big jars filled with silver and gold. The flowers will bloom if the owner will rid himself of half the treasure."

Then Chin Po-wan thanked the Living Kuan-yin and bade her good-bye.

On his return journey, he stopped first at the rich man's house to give him the Living Kuan-yin's answer. In gratitude the rich man gave him half the buried treasure.

Next, Po-wan went to the inn. As he approached, the innkeeper's daughter saw him from the window and called out, "Chin Po-wan! Back already! What did the Living Kuan-yin say?"

Upon hearing his daughter speak at long last, the joyful innkeeper gave her in marriage to Chin Po-wan.

Lastly, Po-wan went to the cliffs by the furiously flowing river to tell the snake what the Living Kuan-yin had said. The grateful snake immediately gave him six of the bright pearls and promptly turned into a magnificent dragon, the remaining pearl in his forehead lighting the headland like a great beacon.

And so it was that Chin Po-wan, that generous and good man, was once more worth a million pieces of gold.

Explain Yourself

VOCABULARY

Answer each question on a separate piece of paper. Be sure to explain your answers.

1. If someone was rude to you, how would you act **accordingly**? Why?

2. How would you help a **destitute** person? Explain.

3. Have you ever done something **inadvertently**? Explain.

4. What plant would you like to **cultivate**? Why?

5. How much paper do you **accumulate** during a normal school day? Explain.

6. Would you take advice from a **sagacious** person? Why or why not?

7. Does an **affluent** person need money? Why or why not?

8. Would a **magnanimous** person be likely to share? Why or why not?

9. Whom would you **solicit** for a birthday gift? Explain.

10. Would you be **undaunted** if your best friend was in trouble? Explain.

accordingly   When you do something accordingly, you do it as a result of something else.

destitute   A destitute person is extremely poor.

inadvertently   If you do something inadvertently, you do it accidentally.

cultivate   If you cultivate something, you take care of it and try to make it grow.

accumulate   When you accumulate things, you gather or collect them over time.

sagacious   Someone who is sagacious is wise and gives good advice.

affluent   Affluent people have a lot of money.

magnanimous
A magnanimous person is very generous.

solicit   When you solicit something, you ask someone for it.

undaunted   If you are undaunted, you aren't worried or discouraged by things that happen.

Take It Further

Complete these sentences on a separate piece of paper.

1. After we won, the coach **accordingly** . . .

2. To avoid being **destitute**, you could . . .

3. During the dance, Julio **inadvertently** . . .

4. In her backyard, Stella **cultivated** . . .

5. During her summer vacation, Monique had time to **accumulate** . . .

6. Dr. Morgan was **sagacious** when it came to . . .

7. I was really surprised when our **affluent** neighbors . . .

8. Charles was **magnanimous**, so on weekends he . . .

9. While Greta was at the mall, she **solicited** her mother for . . .

10. As Jabari swam, he was **undaunted** by . . .

Explore It

One word can take many different forms. Here is another example:

sagacious (adjective)
You can use *sagacious* to describe someone who is wise and gives good advice.

sage (noun)
A sage is a wise person.

sagely (adverb)
Someone who does something sagely does it wisely.

> Work with a partner to create a labeled sketch of a person or character you both consider to be a sage. Use all the words from the word family to describe this person. Be sure to include specific details. Then present your sketch to the class.

133

Barrow, Alaska

"Where Cold Is Ultra Cool!"

If you like nightlife, catch a dogsled and head north to Barrow. From November through January the sun doesn't rise in this arctic wonderland. Still, Barrow is about the lights—the northern lights. It's the best light show you'll ever see.

The 4,500 residents of Barrow will make your stay the best ever. They'll take you bird watching or whale watching. If you're lucky, they'll measure your head like an explorer did back in 1906. The polar bears are not as magnanimous, though, so watch your food supply.

WELCOME to the "Armpit of America"

Come sweat it out at the Festival of the Pit in Battle Mountain, Nevada. During this fabulous festival, townsfolk cultivate their talent for armpit songs, armpit puppetry, and wet, salty armpit sweat. Don't let the festivities bother you, residents are undaunted by the activities.

Unusual U.S. City Names

1. Boring, Oregon
2. Eek, Alaska
3. Embarrass, Wisconsin
4. Greasy, Oklahoma
5. Gripe, Arizona
6. Hardscrabble, North Dakota
7. Oddville, Kentucky
8. Peculiar, Missouri
9. Why, Arizona
10. Yeehaw Junction, Florida

Centralia's ON FIRE!

Ready for some heat? Visit Centralia, Pennsylvania.

Centralia used to be a mining town where workers accumulated large amounts of coal from below the town's surface. In 1962, burning trash set the coal vein on fire. Nothing could stop the flames, so the fire kept burning.

No one lives in Centralia today. Still tourists flock to this destitute ghost town. Why? Where else can you find a 40-year-old fire?

Rev Up Your Writing

The U.S. certainly has some unique places. What is special about your city or town? What would you like to tell the rest of the world about it? Write a brochure for your town. Use as many of the vocabulary words as possible but make sense.

Word Organizer

Copy this graphic organizer onto a separate piece of paper.

Think of words that describe the word *affluent* and write your answers in the ovals. Then give examples of things you would do if you were affluent and write your answers in the boxes. Explain your answers.

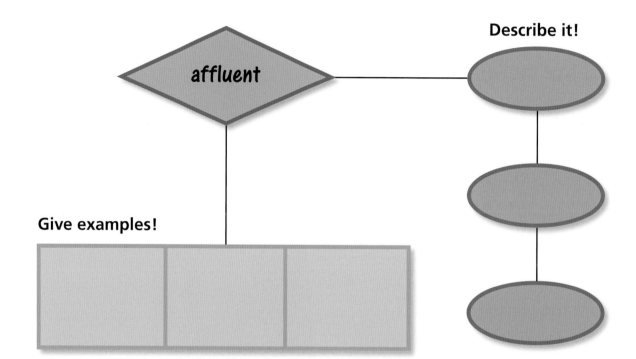

Super Speed

Japan, China, and Germany have trains that can reach speeds of over 300 miles per hour! That's as fast as the wind in the most powerful tornado ever recorded!

These amazing maglev trains get their name from the technology that moves them forward: magnets. The speed of the maglev is possible because the train is actually floating in the air. Powerful magnets line the whole train track. The train itself has metal along the bottom, and the metal is repelled by the magnets. Accordingly, the train floats in the air several inches above the track.

When electrical charges are sent through the magnets, the charge in the magnet sends the metal train forward. Because the train isn't actually touching the track, there's no friction—the track doesn't slow the train down.

Imagine how maglev trains could change the United States. If a maglev were built on the West Coast, for example, it could link many major cities together. You could go from Los Angeles to Seattle in less than an hour. It would be a great form of transportation for businesspeople, tourists, or anyone who wanted to go fast!

Want to see a maglev train in the U.S.? Solicit your government officials with a letter or an email.

magnets

▲ Magnetic forces on the track send the train flying forward.

Movers and Shakers

It's time for a quick look at some new and exciting forms of transportation!

Look How Far We've Come

Technology that we take for granted today wasn't even imagined many years ago. In New York City, before the invention of traffic lights on poles, traffic officers would wear the traffic lights on their bodies! You've heard of people inadvertently running a red light, but have you ever heard of a red light running away?

SAILING THROUGH SPACE? ▶

Some sagacious scientists and researchers have been figuring out ways to sail through outer space. A solar sail is a spacecraft with a large "sail" on it. This sail is really a huge mirror that is pushed forward by light from the sun. Because the sun gives off unlimited energy, a solar sail could travel to Mars and back using only the sun for power!

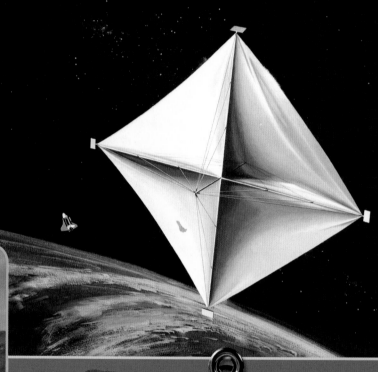

BIKING ON THE HIGHWAY? ▲

Biking in the fast lane of the highway might be possible if everyone owned one of these. This one-of-a-kind bicycle holds the world record for bicycle speed—81 miles per hour. Inventor George Georgiev's bike has already helped him have a more affluent lifestyle. He won $23,000 for breaking the record.

Rev Up Your Writing

You've just read about new technology for transportation. What new kinds of transportation would you like to see in your community? Write a letter to your town council requesting new transportation ideas and explaining why they would benefit your town. Use as many of the vocabulary words as possible but make sense.

Can You Relate?

Copy this graphic organizer onto a separate piece of paper. Match the following words with their related vocabulary word. If a word relates to both vocabulary words, explain why.

frugal A frugal person spends little money and doesn't waste anything.
impecunious Someone who is impecunious has no money.
opulent If something is opulent, it is rich and magnificent.
penury A person living in penury is extremely poor.
prosperous Prosperous people are wealthy, fortunate, or successful.

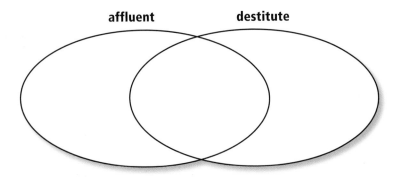

affluent   destitute

In Your Own Words

Respond to one of the following prompts on a separate piece of paper. As you respond, use as many of the vocabulary words as possible. Be creative but make sense!

▶ Describe a wise person you know or have heard about. What have you learned from the person?

▶ Write a newspaper review of a city, restaurant, museum, or concert. Describe what you liked and what you didn't like. Would you recommend it to the readers of your newspaper? Why or why not?

▶ Write about a topic of your choice.

VOCABULARY

accordingly
destitute
inadvertently
cultivate
accumulate
sagacious
affluent
magnanimous
solicit
undaunted

139

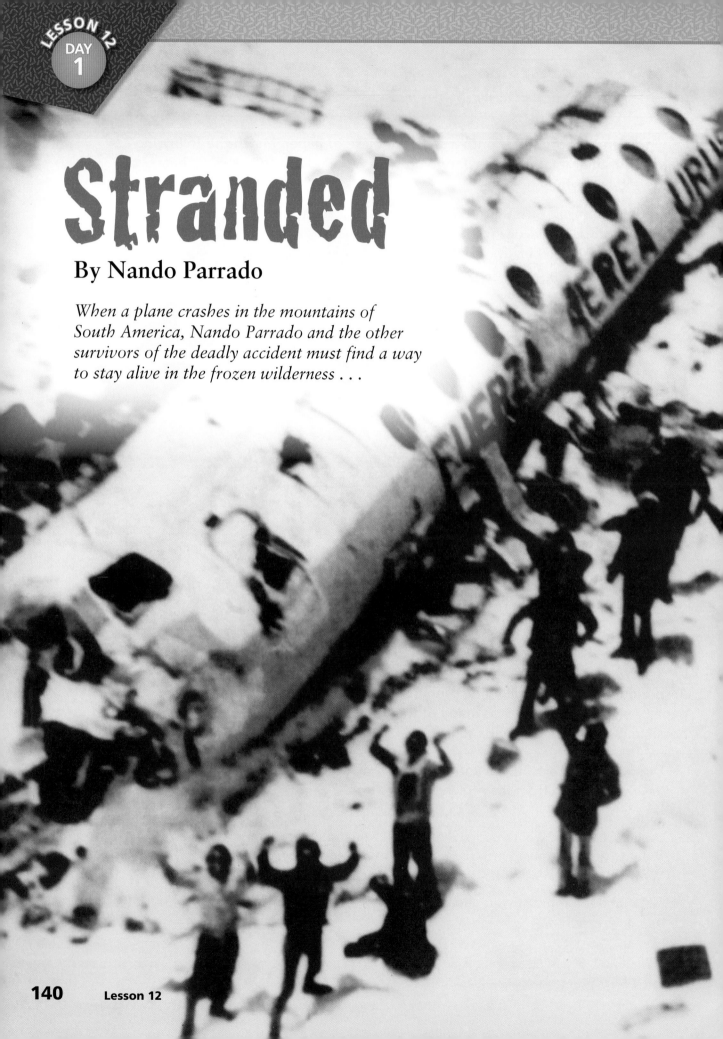

Stranded

By Nando Parrado

*When a plane crashes in the mountains of
South America, Nando Parrado and the other
survivors of the deadly accident must find a way
to stay alive in the frozen wilderness . . .*

In the first hours there was nothing, no fear or sadness, no thought or memory, just a black and perfect silence.

Then light appeared, a thin gray smear of daylight, and I rose to it like a diver swimming to the surface. Consciousness seeped through my brain in a slow bleed;[1] I heard voices and sensed motion all around, but I could see only dark silhouettes and pools of light and shadow. Then, vaguely, I sensed that one of the shadows was hovering over me.

"Nando, *podés oírme?* Can you hear me? Are you OK?"

As I stared dumbly, the shadow gathered itself into a human face. I saw a ragged tangle of dark hair above deep brown eyes. There was kindness in the eyes—this was someone who knew me—but also something else, a wildness, a sense of desperation held in check.[2]

"Come on, Nando, wake up!"

Why am I so cold? Why does my head hurt so badly? I tried to speak these thoughts, but my lips could not form the words. . . .

"Is he awake? Can he hear you?"

"Say something, Nando!"

"Don't give up, Nando. We are here with you. Wake up!"

All I could manage was a hoarse whisper. Then someone spoke slowly in my ear.

"*Nando, el avión se estrelló! Caimos en las montañas.*"

We crashed, he said. The airplane crashed. We fell into the mountains.

"Do you understand me, Nando?"

For more than two days I'd languished in a coma, and I was waking to a nightmare. On Friday the 13th of October, 1972, our plane had smashed into a ridge somewhere in the Argentinian Andes[3] and fallen onto a barren glacier. The twin-engine Fairchild turboprop had been chartered by my rugby[4] team, the Old Christians of Montevideo, Uruguay, to take us to an exhibition match[5] in Santiago, Chile. There were 45 of us on board, including the crew, the team's supporters, and my fellow Old Christians, most of whom I'd played rugby with since we were boys at Catholic school.

FOOTNOTES

. . . .

[1] *Consciousness seeped through my brain in a slow bleed:* I slowly began to be aware of things

[2] *held in check:* controlled

[3] *Argentinian Andes:* a mountain range in South America

[4] *rugby:* a sport similar to American football

[5] *exhibition match:* a game that doesn't affect a team's results in a sports league

Now only 28 remained. My two best friends, Guido Magri and Francisco "Panchito" Abal, were dead. Worse, my mother, Eugenia, and my 19-year-old sister, Susy, had been traveling with us; now, as I lay parched and injured, I learned that my mother had not survived and that Susy was near death.

When I look back, I cannot say why the losses did not destroy me. Grief and panic exploded in my heart with such violence that I feared I would go mad. But then a thought formed, in a voice so lucid and detached it could have been someone whispering in my ear. The voice said, *Do not cry. Tears waste salt. You will need the salt to survive.*

I was astounded at the calmness of this thought and the cold-bloodedness[6] of the voice that spoke it. Not cry for my mother? I am stranded in the Andes, freezing; my sister may be dying; my skull is in pieces! I should not cry?

Do not cry. . . .

* * * * * * * *

Never had I felt so terribly alone. I was 22 years old. My mother was dead. My sister was dead. My best friends had been sucked from the plane in flight, or were buried outside. Most of us were untested young men between the ages of 18 and 21, lost in the wilderness, hungry, injured, and freezing. With stinging clarity I felt the brute power of the mountains, saw the complete absence of warmth or mercy or softness in the landscape, and for the first time, I knew with certainty that I would die.

But then I thought of my father again, and as I stared out at those ragged peaks, I felt my love for him tugging at me like a lifeline, drawing me toward those merciless slopes. *I will come home*, I vowed to him. *I promise you, I will not die here!*

From my very first hours in the mountains, I felt, deep in my bones, the immediacy of the danger that surrounded us. Nothing in the late-winter Andes welcomed human life. The cold tormented us. The thin air starved our lungs. The unfiltered sun blinded us and blistered our lips and skin, and the snow was so deep that we could not venture far without sinking to our hips. . . .

FOOTNOTES
....
[6] *cold-bloodedness:* a lack of emotion or feeling

If not for our team captain, Marcelo Pérez, we wouldn't have lasted a night. Marcelo was a wing forward[7]—very fast, very brave, and a leader we would trust with our lives. After the crash, as the stupefied[8] survivors staggered about in disbelief, Marcelo had organized the uninjured into a search party to free the dozens of passengers still trapped in the heaps of tangled seats in the plane. Roberto Canessa and Gustavo Zerbino, two players who were also in medical school, had done their best to tend to the injuries, some of which were grisly[9]. . . .

As darkness fell, Marcelo turned the Fairchild into a makeshift[10] shelter, stacking loose seats and luggage in the gaping hole left by the tail, then packing the gaps with snow. The living were jammed into a cramped space on the litter-strewn floor measuring no more than eight by ten feet.

Marcelo's wall kept us from freezing, but in the coming nights we suffered terribly from the cold. We had cigarette lighters and could easily have lit a fire, but there was little combustible material. We burned all our paper money—almost $7,500 went up in smoke—and found enough scrap wood to fuel two or three small fires, but the brief luxury of warmth only made the cold seem worse. . . .

By the end of the first week, with no sign of rescue, we began to solve our most pressing problems.[11] Roberto devised ingenious hammocks for the most injured and improvised flimsy blankets from the plane's thin nylon seat covers. Thirst was not an issue, thanks to Adolfo "Fito" Strauch, a quiet, serious former player who had improvised snow-melting basins from square aluminum sheets he found lining the bottoms of the seats.

But we were beginning to starve. One of the first things Marcelo had done was gather everything edible from scattered suitcases or the cabin. There wasn't much—chocolate bars and other snacks. . . . Each meal was nothing more than a small square of chocolate or a dab of jam. . . . It wasn't enough to satisfy anyone's hunger, but as a ritual it gave us strength.

FOOTNOTES

[7] *wing forward:* a rugby position played by someone big and strong
[8] *stupefied:* confused and amazed
[9] *grisly:* horrible and disgusting
[10] *makeshift:* temporary
[11] *pressing problems:* most important and serious problems

One morning, I found myself standing outside the fuselage,[12] looking down at a single chocolate-covered peanut cradled in my palm. This was the final morsel of food I would be given, and with a sad, almost miserly desperation, I was determined to make it last. I slowly sucked the chocolate off the peanut, then slipped it into the pocket of my slacks. The next day I carefully separated the peanut halves, slipping one half back into my pocket and placing the other in my mouth. I sucked gently on it for hours, allowing myself only a tiny piece now and then. I did the same on the third day, and when I'd finally nibbled the peanut down to nothing, there was no food left at all.

FOOTNOTES
····················
12 *fuselage:* the body of an airplane

Explain Yourself

Answer each question on a separate piece of paper. Be sure to explain your answers.

1. Would you help a friend who was **languishing**? Why or why not?

2. Would you like to visit a **barren** place on your next vacation? Why or why not?

3. If your teacher explained a science experiment **lucidly**, how would your experiment go? Why?

4. Would you want to drive a **combustible** car? Why or why not?

5. If your brother or sister asked to borrow some money from you, would you be **miserly**? Why or why not?

6. How could you **bolster** your best friend's mood?

7. What would you do if there were a **dearth** of good food in the cafeteria?

8. Think of a character from a book or movie who ended up in a **dire** situation. Describe the character's situation.

9. Why might your friend sound **incoherent** on the phone? Explain.

10. Have you ever had an **insatiable** desire for something? Explain.

VOCABULARY

languish When you languish through something, you suffer and become weak.

barren A barren place is empty, dry, or unable to grow things.

lucid Something lucid is plain and clear or easy to understand.

combustible If something is combustible, you can burn it easily.

miserly A miserly person is stingy and doesn't want to give away anything.

bolster If you bolster something, you support it and make it stronger.

dearth When there is a dearth of something, there is not enough of it.

dire If a situation is dire, it is extremely bad and it seems like there is no hope.

incoherent If someone or something is incoherent, it is not clear and is difficult to understand.

insatiable Someone who is insatiable can't get enough and is never satisfied.

Take It Further

Complete these sentences on a separate piece of paper.

1. Last winter, I was **languishing** because . . .

2. Because the street was **barren**, Ana . . .

3. Troy's description of his trip to India was so **lucid** that . . .

4. When we went camping, Dad collected **combustible** things to . . .

5. I could tell that my grandfather was **miserly** when he . . .

6. Lucy **bolstered** the walls of the old shed by . . .

7. There was a **dearth** of good music on my favorite radio station, so . . .

8. With only ten seconds left in the game, Taeko knew the situation was **dire** because . . .

9. I started talking **incoherently** when I saw . . .

10. Dmitri was **insatiable**, so after dinner he . . .

LESSON 12
DAY 4

Explore It

Remember how you can attach a prefix to the beginning of a word to change its meaning? For example, if you attach the prefix *in–* to the word *appropriate*, you can tell that *in–* can mean "not."

Your teacher will give you and a partner a sheet of paper with the prefix *in–* written on it. With your partner, decide who will be the actor and who will be the "prefixer." You'll each have a chance to play both roles. When the prefixer holds the sheet of paper in the air, the actor should start acting incoherently. When the prefixer lowers the paper, the actor should be coherent.

Now switch roles and try the same activity using the word *insatiable*.

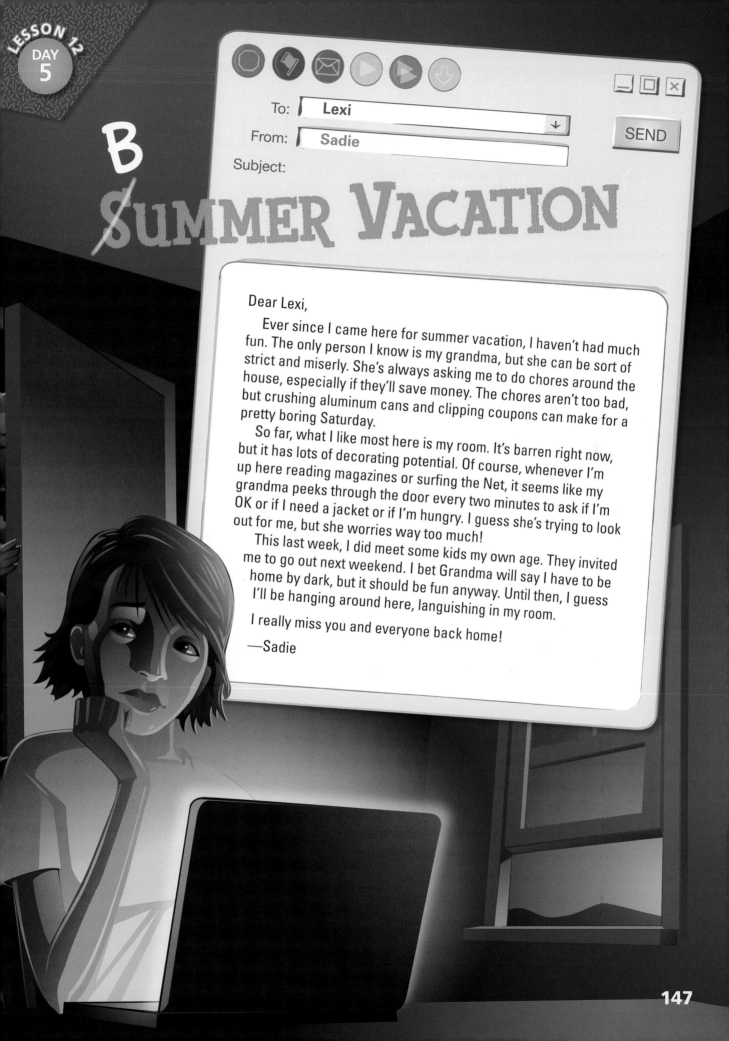

B

SUMMER VACATION

To: Lexi

From: Sadie

Subject:

SEND

Dear Lexi,

Ever since I came here for summer vacation, I haven't had much fun. The only person I know is my grandma, but she can be sort of strict and miserly. She's always asking me to do chores around the house, especially if they'll save money. The chores aren't too bad, but crushing aluminum cans and clipping coupons can make for a pretty boring Saturday.

So far, what I like most here is my room. It's barren right now, but it has lots of decorating potential. Of course, whenever I'm up here reading magazines or surfing the Net, it seems like my grandma peeks through the door every two minutes to ask if I'm OK or if I need a jacket or if I'm hungry. I guess she's trying to look out for me, but she worries way too much!

This last week, I did meet some kids my own age. They invited me to go out next weekend. I bet Grandma will say I have to be home by dark, but it should be fun anyway. Until then, I guess I'll be hanging around here, languishing in my room.

I really miss you and everyone back home!

—Sadie

My Insatiable Family

a song by Rosie Bordeaux

When it comes time to eat, we gather 'round,
no matter what we are doing in what part of town.
Eighteen in our family, plus Gram and Gramps makes it twenty.
Our meals take a while; of food there is plenty.

chorus:
Sometimes we're cranky, but it's 'cause we're hungry;
sometimes we're noisy, but it's just tummies grumblin'.
Cooking our meals may seem like a feat.
If there's one thing our family does well, it is eat!

When we finally finish, the situation looks dire;
there are so many dishes, just looking I'm tired.
But I know it's my duty; I didn't cook, so I'll clean.
Plus it takes so much energy—it's why I'm so lean!

chorus (two times)

Rev Up Your Writing

You've just read about two people who are making the best of less-than-ideal situations. Write about a time you made the best of a situation that wasn't ideal. What was the situation? How did you handle it? Use as many of the vocabulary words as possible but make sense.

Word Organizer

Copy this graphic organizer onto a separate piece of paper.

List words that mean almost the same thing as *lucid* and write your answers in the web.

Then tell about a time when you saw or heard something lucid.

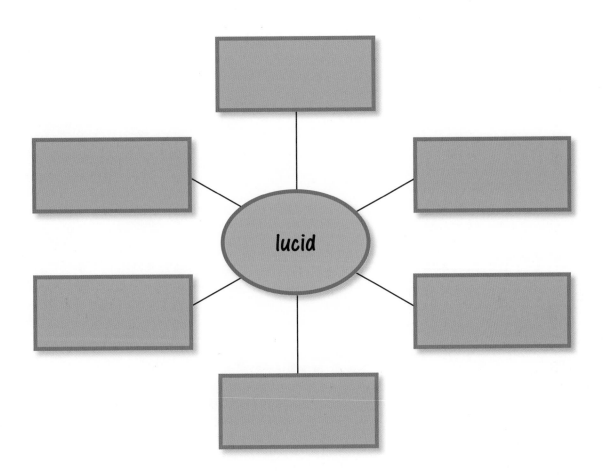

My SPACE-CRAZY Family

When it comes to outer space, I'm the odd one out in my family. My dad is a space nut. He's always outside with his telescope, talking incoherently about comets. It drives me crazy, but my sister Selena loves it. Dad and Selena talk about space so much that sometimes I wish they'd just get in a rocket and go there.

Last week, things got totally out of control. It was 3 A.M. I was asleep in my warm bed. Suddenly, something attacked!

"Selena!" I yelled. "Leave me alone!"

I heard Dad's lucid voice behind Selena. "Time to get up, Tony!" he said happily.

"Are you crazy?" I asked. "Is this a joke?"

It wasn't. Dad wanted me to see a meteor shower. "I don't even know what that *is*," I grumbled.

"It's like a whole bunch of shooting stars," said Selena. OK, but even if you wanted to watch a bunch of combustible things in the sky, why would you do it at 3 A.M.?

Dad marched us down the road and into a field. I looked at the sky. Not only were there no meteors, there was a dearth of stars in general; a giant cloud covered the entire night sky.

"Oh no," Dad said.

I was furious. Now I was wide-awake, I was cold, and the grass had made my pajamas wet. Why couldn't my family love something normal, like football? I started walking home so fast that I almost didn't see the streak of light shoot across the sky.

I stopped walking and looked up. The cloud was disappearing. There was another streak! Then another right behind it! I gasped. They were definitely meteors.

Dad smiled at me. "What do you think?" he asked.

"Eh, they're OK," I said. I wasn't quite ready to let him know I thought they were amazing.

Fascinating Space Facts

Until the 16th century, people thought Earth was the center of the universe. They believed that Earth stayed still while the planets and the sun all traveled around it.

In the 1970s, scientists wanted to bolster the possibility of making contact with alien life forms, so they sent messages inside a rocket that is still flying through interstellar space today. Among the symbols and drawings sent were pictures of humans and a map of Earth's location.

Feeling a little dusty? Maybe it's because scientists have guessed that about 1,000 tons of dust from space land on Earth every day!

Even though they're not alive, stars have a life cycle a lot like plants and animals do. They are born, grow old, and die over the course of millions of years. Some stars end their lives as black holes.

Outer space doesn't look much like a trash can, but more than 110,000 pieces of trash are circling Earth. They're bits and pieces left over from past missions into space—spaceship parts, trash bags, and even gloves!

Don't make any plans for five billion years from now. That's when the sun will burn out and destroy Earth in the process!

Did You Know?

The universe isn't the same size it used to be. In the 20th century, scientist Edwin Hubble discovered that the universe is getting bigger and bigger.

Rev Up Your Writing

Selena and Tony's dad love studying outer space. Does space interest you? Why or why not? Would you ever want to be an astronaut or a space tourist? Explain. Use as many of the vocabulary words as possible but make sense.

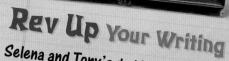

151

Can You Relate?

Copy this graphic organizer onto a separate piece of paper. Match the following words with their related vocabulary word. If a word relates to more than one vocabulary word, explain why.

atrophy   If something atrophies, it shrinks, gets weaker, or wastes away.
befuddle   If you are befuddled, you are very confused.
decrepit   Something that is decrepit is old, weak, or falling apart.
garble   If you garble a message, you scramble it or confuse its meaning.
malady   A malady is an illness.

languish	dire	incoherent

In Your Own Words

Respond to one of the following prompts on a separate piece of paper. As you respond, use as many of the vocabulary words as possible. Be creative but make sense!

▶ Write about a time when a family member or close friend taught you something new. What did you learn? What was interesting or surprising about it? How did it change your relationship with the other person?

▶ Imagine you are a villain from one of your favorite books, movies, games, or shows. Write a short autobiography about your life. Explain your side of the story and tell the world why you aren't as terrible as everyone thinks you are.

▶ Write about a topic of your choice.

VOCABULARY

languish
barren
lucid
combustible
miserly
bolster
dearth
dire
incoherent
insatiable

from
The Story of My Life

By Helen Keller

Left deaf and blind by illness when she was only 19 months old, Helen Keller lived cut off from the rest of the world by her inability to communicate. Then one day a stranger arrived who would help her break through.

The most important day I remember in all my life is the one on which my teacher, Anne Mansfield Sullivan, came to me. I am filled with wonder when I consider the immeasurable contrast between the two lives which it connects. It was the third of March, 1887, three months before I was seven years old.

On the afternoon of that eventful day, I stood on the porch, dumb,[1] expectant. I guessed vaguely from my mother's signs and from the hurrying to and fro[2] in the house that something unusual was about to happen, so I went to the door and waited on the steps. The afternoon sun penetrated the mass of honeysuckle that covered the porch, and fell on my upturned face. My fingers lingered[3] almost unconsciously on the familiar leaves and blossoms which had just come forth to greet the sweet southern spring. I did not know what the future held of marvel or surprise for me. Anger and bitterness had preyed upon me continually for weeks and a deep languor[4] had succeeded this passionate struggle.

Have you ever been at sea in a dense fog, when it seemed as if a tangible white darkness shut you in, and the great ship, tense and anxious, groped her way toward the shore with plummet and sounding-line,[5] and you waited with beating heart for something to happen? I was like that ship before my education began, only I was without compass or sounding-line, and had no way of knowing how near the harbor was. "Light! give me light!" was the wordless cry of my soul, and the light of love shone on me in that very hour.

I felt approaching footsteps. I stretched out my hand as I supposed to my mother. Someone took it, and I was caught up and held close in the arms of her who had come to reveal all things to me, and, more than all things else, to love me.

FOOTNOTES
. . . .
1 *dumb:* unable to speak
2 *to and fro:* back and forth
3 *lingered:* stayed
4 *languor:* a lack of energy or strength
5 *plummet and sounding-line:* tools used to measure ocean depth

The morning after my teacher came she led me into her room and gave me a doll. The little blind children at the Perkins Institution had sent it and Laura Bridgman had dressed it; but I did not know this until afterward. When I had played with it a little while, Miss Sullivan slowly spelled into my hand[6] the word "d-o-l-l." I was at once interested in this finger play and tried to imitate it. When I finally succeeded in making the letters correctly I was flushed with childish pleasure and pride. Running downstairs to my mother I held up my hand and made the letters for doll. I did not know that I was spelling a word or even that words existed; I was simply making my fingers go in monkey-like imitation. In the days that followed I learned to spell in this uncomprehending way a great many words, among them *pin*, *hat*, *cup* and a few verbs like *sit*, *stand* and *walk*. But my teacher had been with me several weeks before I understood that everything has a name.

One day, while I was playing with my new doll, Miss Sullivan put my big rag doll into my lap also, spelled "d-o-l-l" and tried to make me understand that "d-o-l-l" applied to both. Earlier in the day we had had a tussle[7] over the words "m-u-g" and "w-a-t-e-r." Miss Sullivan had tried to impress it upon me that "m-u-g" is *mug* and that "w-a-t-e-r" is *water*, but I persisted in confounding the two. In despair she had dropped the subject for the time, only to renew it at the first opportunity. I became impatient at her repeated attempts and, seizing the new doll, I dashed it upon the floor. I was keenly delighted when I felt the fragments of the broken doll at my feet. Neither sorrow nor regret followed my passionate outburst. I had not loved the doll. In the still, dark world in which I lived there was no strong sentiment or tenderness. I felt my teacher sweep the fragments to one side of the hearth,[8] and I had a sense of satisfaction that the cause of my discomfort was removed. She brought me my hat, and I knew I was going out into the warm sunshine. This thought, if a wordless sensation may be called a thought, made me hop and skip with pleasure.

FOOTNOTES

6 *spelled into my hand:* formed the letters using sign language

7 *tussle:* a struggle or fight

8 *hearth:* the floor of a fireplace

We walked down the path to the well-house, attracted by the fragrance of the honeysuckle with which it was covered. Someone was drawing water and my teacher placed my hand under the spout. As the cool stream gushed over one hand she spelled into the other the word *water*, first slowly, then rapidly. I stood still, my whole attention fixed upon the motions of her fingers. Suddenly I felt a misty consciousness as of something forgotten—a thrill of returning thought; and somehow the mystery of language was revealed to me. I knew then that "w-a-t-e-r" meant the wonderful cool something that was flowing over my hand. That living word awakened my soul, gave it light, hope, joy, set it free! There were barriers still, it is true, but barriers that could in time be swept away.

I left the well-house eager to learn. Everything had a name, and each name gave birth to a new thought. As we returned to the house every object which I touched seemed to quiver with life. That was because I saw everything with the strange, new sight that had come to me. On entering the door I remembered the doll I had broken. I felt my way to the hearth and picked up the pieces. I tried vainly to put them together. Then my eyes filled with tears; for I realized what I had done, and for the first time I felt repentance and sorrow.

I learned a great many new words that day. I do not remember what they all were; but I do know that *mother*, *father*, *sister*, *teacher* were among them—words that were to make the world blossom for me, "like Aaron's rod,[9] with flowers." It would have been difficult to find a happier child than I was as I lay in my crib at the close of that eventful day and lived over the joys it had brought me, and for the first time longed for a new day to come.

FOOTNOTES

9 *Aaron's rod:* a tall, densely flowered plant

Explain Yourself

VOCABULARY

Answer each question on a separate piece of paper. Be sure to explain your answers.

1. What might you be **expectant** for at your birthday party? Explain.

2. What are three things that you do **unconsciously**? Explain.

3. How would you feel if you were attacked by something that wasn't **tangible**? Why?

4. What would make your sports team **despair**? Explain.

5. What are some common signs that someone is feeling **repentant**? Explain.

6. Would you want to have a **benevolent** teacher? Why or why not?

7. Would you feel **jubilant** about getting a bad grade? Why or why not?

8. What kind of movies **intrigue** you? Why?

9. Would you want to **decipher** a strange language? Why or why not?

10. What **revitalizes** you after school? Explain.

expectant   When you are expectant, you think something is about to happen.

unconsciously   If you do something unconsciously, you do it without being aware that you are doing it.

tangible   Something that is tangible can be touched.

despair   When you despair, you feel like there is no hope.

repentance   Repentance is a feeling of sorrow and regret for something you did that was wrong.

benevolent   Benevolent people are kind and patient.

jubilant   Someone who is jubilant feels great joy and excitement.

intrigue   When someone or something intrigues you, it fascinates you and makes you curious.

decipher   If you decipher something, you figure out something that is difficult to understand.

revitalize   When you are revitalized, you feel as though you have been given new life and energy.

157

Take It Further

Complete these sentences on a separate piece of paper.

1. After dinner, we waited **expectantly** for . . .

2. I was so embarrassed when I **unconsciously** . . .

3. The **tangible** reward for finding my guitar will be . . .

4. I **despaired** when my friend told me . . .

5. Out of **repentance**, I called my friend and . . .

6. For the weekend, our **benevolent** grandfather . . .

7. Marina was **jubilant** after she was declared . . .

8. The astronauts were **intrigued** when they . . .

9. It took Jesse three hours to **decipher** . . .

10. To **revitalize** themselves, the basketball team . . .

Explore It

How much do you know about where the words you use came from? For example, did you know that the prefix in *benevolent (bene–)* comes from the Latin word *bene*, meaning "good"?

Working with others, take what you now know about the prefix *bene–* and create other words that could have the same prefix. For example, what would you call a good sandwich? How about a good parent? Have fun and be ready to share your new word creations with the class!

Bonus: Use a dictionary and find other words that use the prefix bene–. *How many examples can you find?*

Teen Entrepreneurs Hit the Big Time!

These intriguing people started their successful businesses as teens. Could you do the same?

Monique Alleyne

At age 17, Monique Alleyne opened Alleyne Studios in her home in Washington, DC. Even though she only worked on Sundays, in one year Alleyne made as much as $8,000 giving piano lessons to six clients between the ages of 6 and 65!

Weina Scott & Jake Fischer

Seventeen-year-old Weina Scott and sixteen-year-old Jake Fischer created Switchpod.com, a Web site that allows users to upload and share audio and video programs. Several months later, Scott and Fischer sold Switchpod.com to another company for stock worth $200,000.

Dr. Farrah Gray

At age 6, Farrah Gray began his career in business going door-to-door selling homemade body lotion and bookends. By the time he was 16, Farrah Gray had started several new businesses, including a phone card company, a postal supply franchise, a teen-centered radio talk show, and a food company called Farr-Out Foods (whose best selling product was strawberry-vanilla syrup that produced more than 1.5 million orders). By that time, Farrah Gray was a self-made millionaire!

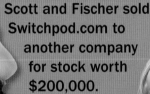

◀ Thousands of people like Lora use Switchpod.com everyday.

159

$$$ CHA-CHING
MAKE IT YOUR BIZ!

Thinking about starting a business? Interested in being your own boss? Consider these great tips and answer the questions to start your own business. Good luck!

1 Where can you get some ideas for starting a business?

- $ Benevolent family, friends, teachers, or counselors
- $ The Internet
- $ Personal experiences, interests, or hobbies—whatever intrigues you

2 Are you willing to sacrifice your time? Answer the following questions to find out:

- $ Will you have time to advertise and create tangible examples of your product or service?
- $ Will the business affect your success in school?
- $ Will you be willing to give up sports or time with your friends if you need to?

3 Before you start your business, decipher your reasons for wanting to go into business. Some reasons are:

- $ You want to make your own money and lots of it!
- $ You want to be your own boss.
- $ You simply want to put your talent to good use.

4 Who's your customer? Do some research and answer the following questions:

- $ Can you create a demand for your business?
- $ Will your product or service fulfill a need?
- $ Who or what is your competition?

5 Finally, don't despair! Before you make a decision, answer the following questions:

- $ What do you like to do?
- $ What kind of skills do you have?
- $ What do others say you are good at?

Rev Up Your Writing

Creating a successful business takes thought and time. Using notes from the questions above, create a plan for your own business. What kind of business would you start? What would you do to start making your business a success? Use as many vocabulary words as possible but make sense.

Word Organizer

Copy this graphic organizer onto a separate piece of paper.

Jubilant is near the hot end of the Word-O-Meter. Think of words that would be hotter or colder. Write your answers in the boxes. Explain your answers.

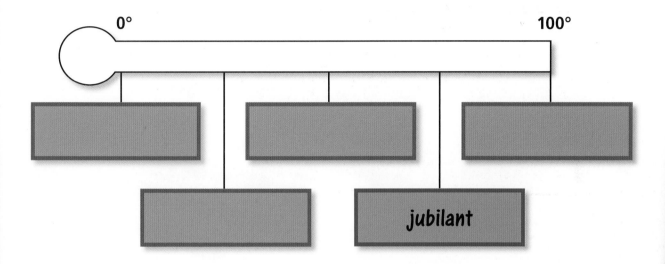

0°   100°

jubilant

"Life will always be intriguing through the eyes of a jubilant person."
—Anonymous

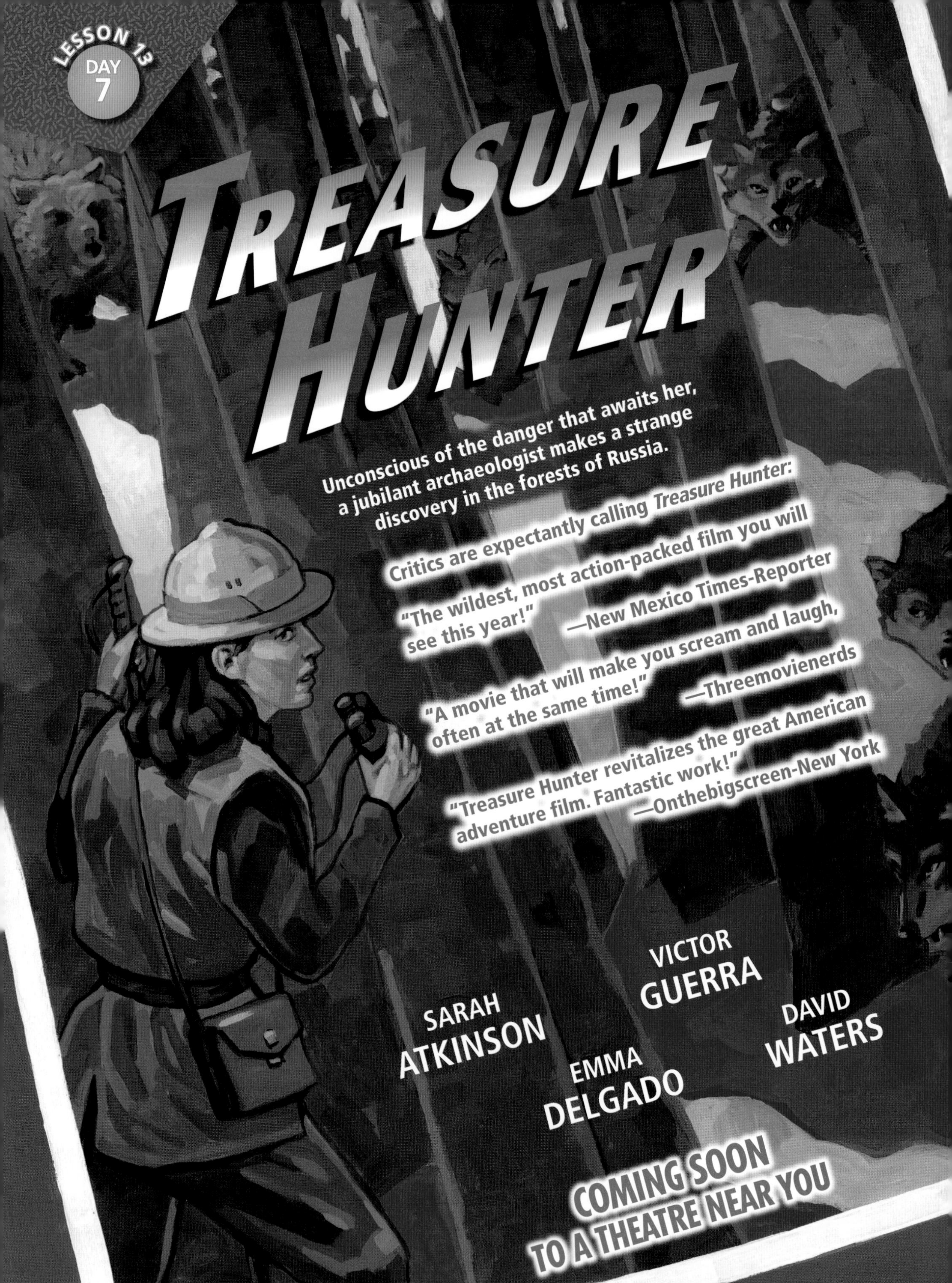

TREASURE HUNTER

Unconscious of the danger that awaits her, a jubilant archaeologist makes a strange discovery in the forests of Russia.

Critics are expectantly calling *Treasure Hunter*:

"The wildest, most action-packed film you will see this year!"
—New Mexico Times-Reporter

"A movie that will make you scream and laugh, often at the same time!"
—Threemovienerds

"*Treasure Hunter* revitalizes the great American adventure film. Fantastic work!"
—Onthebigscreen-New York

SARAH
ATKINSON

VICTOR
GUERRA

EMMA
DELGADO

DAVID
WATERS

COMING SOON
TO A THEATRE NEAR YOU

A WORD WITH
Emma Delgado

We here at Movie Time were lucky enough to catch up with the star of *Treasure Hunter*, Emma Delgado.

Movie Time: Where did you film *Treasure Hunter*?

Emma Delgado: We filmed some of the scenes on location in the forests of northern Russia and the cave scenes on a movie set in Hollywood. At first, I couldn't believe they were making me go to Russia. The weather was extreme and the Mexican food was terrible. Still I must repent for the way I treated people. They were really very nice and the forests were beautiful.

Movie Time: Tell us about the stunts you did in this movie.

Emma Delgado: The most dangerous stunt I did involved climbing a tree so that I could spy on some unsuspecting archaeologists. I was halfway up the tree when my leg cramped up, sending me plunging to the ground. I couldn't believe the director made me do such a dangerous stunt—it destroyed my fabulous hairdo!

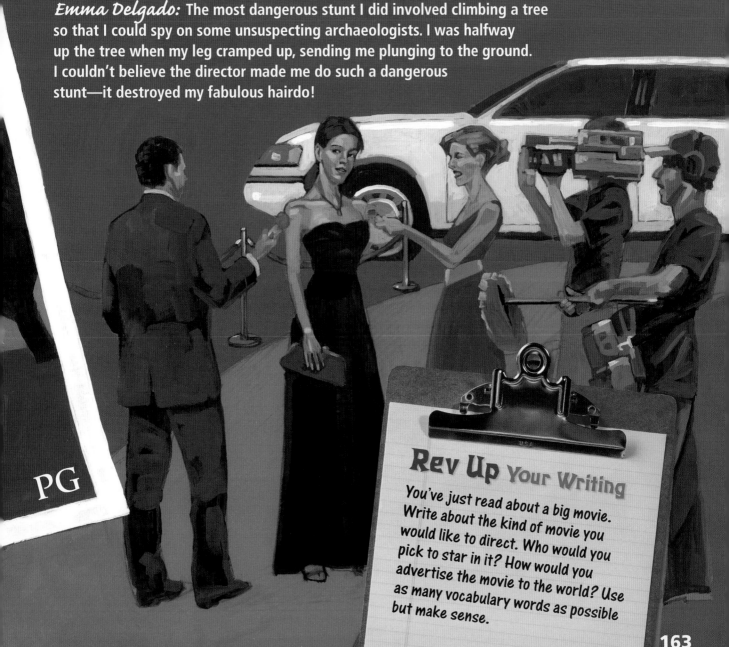

PG

Rev Up Your Writing

You've just read about a big movie. Write about the kind of movie you would like to direct. Who would you pick to star in it? How would you advertise the movie to the world? Use as many vocabulary words as possible but make sense.

Can You Relate?

Copy this graphic organizer onto a separate piece of paper. Match the following words with their related vocabulary word. If a word relates to more than one vocabulary word, explain why.

alluring   When something is alluring, it is very attractive and charming.

apprehend   When you apprehend something, you understand or capture it.

hieroglyphics   Hieroglyphics are an ancient style of writing that used pictures for words.

perceive   When you perceive something, you notice it, especially when it is not easy to notice.

tantalizing   Something that is tantalizing is very interesting and tempting.

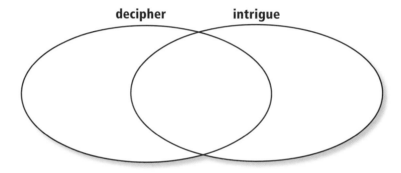

decipher   intrigue

In Your Own Words

VOCABULARY

expectant
unconsciously
tangible
despair
repentance
benevolent
jubilant
intrigue
decipher
revitalize

Respond to one of the following prompts on a separate piece of paper. As you respond, use as many of the vocabulary words as possible. Be creative but make sense!

▶ Write about a time when you or someone you know taught another person how to do something. Was teaching easier or harder than you expected? How did the experience make you feel? What did you learn?

▶ Write a review of one of your favorite or least favorite movies. Describe the plot and the characters using words that convey your opinion of the movie. Persuade people to either see or avoid the movie.

▶ Write about a topic of your choice.

Animal Liberation

By Genny Lim
Illustrated by Meryl Treatner

*On a trip to a Chinese market, a woman buys
food for the soul, not for the stomach.*

Other than a chickadee which I had bought from
a pick-up truck vendor many, many years ago
I had never purchased a live animal

Today I went to Chinatown and parked on the south end of Grant
I walked down the street combing[1] the poultry shops for a live duck
Most of the old markets had been shut down
under pressure from the Animal Humane Society[2]

No more cages piled high on the sidewalks with the odor of fowl
or loose feathers dusting the already acrid air
Wooden crates jammed with roosters, hens and pigeons
Barrels of live frogs and turtles had been replaced by
Spanking new tourist emporiums[3] spilling silk brocades,[4]
Chinaware and hand-carved deities[5] from their over-stocked shelves

I make my way through the crowds into one market displaying
Roasted ducks hanging upside-down
I ask the proprietress,[6] "Do you have any live ducks?"
She points next door

I walk into a long, narrow room with wooden cages kept behind a
    glass partition[7]
"Do you have any live ducks?" I ask the old poker-faced[8] poultry man
Without blinking, he asks, "How many?"
I ask him "How much for one?" in Chinese
He answers, "*Sup-yih-gah-bun!*"

Twelve dollars and fifty cents for the life of a duck?
I reply, "One!"

He turns around and opens the door to one of the crates
and reaches in and pulls out a big, speckled brown duck
He grabs it by the neck and ties its feet together
Then he stuffs the bird into a paper bag punctured with holes at the top
I pay him my money and he hands over the bag

FOOTNOTES
....
[1] *combing:* searching
    through
[2] *Animal Humane
    Society:* an animal
    rights organization
[3] *emporiums:* stores
[4] *brocades:* fabrics with
    complex designs
[5] *deities:* gods and
    goddesses
[6] *proprietress:* a store
    owner
[7] *partition:* a divider or
    separator
[8] *poker-faced:* showing
    no emotions

I am so excited my heart is racing[9] all the way out the door
I clutch the duck's warm body against my chest and
It feels like that of my baby before she had grown into a beautiful
   young lady
Hard to believe nineteen years had passed since
I had held her tiny body to me just like this

I walk the length of Grant Avenue with my contraband[10]
I'm relieved I don't have a ticket and place the duck in the back
   of the car
I head out to the park with a heightened awareness of my sudden
   new surroundings
The buildings are unusually vivid, the pedestrians unusually alive
I park at Stow Lake and walk around till I find a spot
near the reeds obscured[11] from view

I walk down the embankment[12] with my heart throbbing
I open the bag half expecting the duck to bite me
But she sits there calmly and patiently as I untie
the tight band of wire wrapped around her legs

Talking to her gently as I free her
I'm afraid to upset her by picking her up so
I turn the bag upside down and literally pour her into the water
She tumbles into the lake and as soon as her body makes contact
   with liquid
There is instant recognition
She dives into the pool and emerges with her feathers wet and
   glistening
She spreads her wings wide for the first time and quacks with joy
She dives in and out again and again
Baptizing[13] her entire body with miraculous water

My heart sings[14] to see this once captive duck
Frolic in the lake, diving and dancing, flapping her wings
as flocks of black guinea hens pass by in cool demeanor
And proud mallards[15] observe their new member with calm disinterest
She quacks and cavorts like a prisoner released from death row

I sigh, never taking my eyes off her for a moment
Until she is joined by an identical speckled brown duck
They swim together pass the boaters, pass the reeds beyond sight
"Free!" I breathe, "at last!" One life saved for another one lost

Good-bye my darling, Danielle!
May your consciousness leap into the vast and familiar depths of
    Sukhavati[16]
And may you reunite quickly with the hosts of enlightened[17] beings
Who have gone on ahead of you and who will soon follow!

Explain Yourself

Answer each question on a separate piece of paper. Be sure to explain your answers.

1. What would you do if the cafeteria food tasted **acrid**? Explain.

2. Why might someone **puncture** an ear? Explain.

3. If your friend said, "you're pulling my leg" would you take that **literally**? Explain.

4. What kind of **demeanor** does your best friend have? Explain.

5. What would you think if you saw a baseball team **cavorting** during a game? Explain.

6. How would your mother react if you **emancipated** a pet mouse? Why or why not?

7. What is the most **fortuitous** thing that has ever happened to you?

8. How could you **metaphorically** describe a friend who loves to swim?

9. What would a **dappled** horse look like?

10. Would you **reconcile** yourself to losing a softball game? Why or why not?

VOCABULARY

acrid An acrid smell or taste is unpleasantly strong and bitter.

puncture If you puncture something, you make a small hole in it.

literally If something is said to have literally happened, it actually happened the way it was described.

demeanor Your demeanor is your appearance or behavior.

cavort Someone or something that cavorts leaps about in a playful and excited way.

emancipate When you emancipate someone or something, you set it free.

fortuitous You say it is fortuitous when something good happens just by chance.

metaphorical You are being metaphorical when you describe something by using images or symbols.

dappled Something that is dappled has a lot of spots on it.

reconcile If you reconcile yourself to a situation, you accept it as it is.

Take It Further

Complete these sentences on a separate piece of paper.

1. When Amelia smelled something **acrid**, she . . .

2. Hassan **punctured** the raft when he . . .

3. Rick didn't **literally** mean that Kim should . . .

4. Irina's **demeanor** was . . .

5. My puppy started **cavorting** when . . .

6. Toby was relieved when he was **emancipated** from . . .

7. Pao couldn't believe how **fortuitous** it was that . . .

8. Paige was just being **metaphorical** when she said . . .

9. I accidentally **dappled** my new shirt with . . .

10. Nora tried, but she couldn't **reconcile** herself to the fact that . . .

Explore It

If you want to tell your friends a story, you can tell it either literally or metaphorically. Both literal language and metaphorical language can be useful in different situations. A news reporter writes as literally as possible so that everyone knows exactly what happened. A poet writes metaphors to help readers imagine something that would be boring or complicated if it were explained literally.

On the top of a blank sheet of paper, write a metaphorical description of a friend or family member. For example, you could write: "Elsa is a bird when she sings." On the bottom of the paper, write the literal meaning of your metaphorical description: "Elsa has a beautiful singing voice." In the blank space in the middle of the paper, draw a picture illustrating the metaphorical description as if it were literal. In this case, you'd draw your friend Elsa as a bird. Check out your classmates' descriptions and see if they've come up with any crazy pictures of you!

The Sky Painter

A myth

Long ago, a boy named Ku lived with his father, Day. Their house sat on top of the highest mountain. When Ku wasn't careful, he bumped his head on the sky.

Day was a painter. Each morning, Day dipped his brush into blue paint and swept it across the sky. The sky turned blue, and the morning began. After many hours, Day picked up a cloth and rubbed the paint away. Each morning Day painted the sky, and each night he scrubbed it clean.

When Ku was fourteen, he asked if he could help paint the sky. "You're too young," said Day, "and I don't want you cavorting across the sky." Ku couldn't believe his ears. If Day thought Ku would reconcile himself to being a child forever, he was wrong.

That night, Ku crept outside and brushed blue paint across the sky. Instantly, it was morning. It was so easy! He began to paint faster. Everything looked perfect.

Then flies got stuck in the paint, dappling the sky with black spots. Ku painted over them, but the spots grew into a huge black smudge. Soon he ran out of blue paint. Panicked, he painted stripes in other colors—purple, pink, and orange. Finally, he wiped everything clean.

When Ku went home, Day was furious.

Suddenly, the door swung open. Hundreds of people stood outside.

"We loved your new patterns!" they cried. "We want to see colored stripes every evening. Please keep painting them!"

Day looked surprised. Then he smiled. "All right," he said, "but I'll need my son to help."

Hero of NEWPORT HARBOR

Ida Lewis probably never dreamed she'd be a hero. She was born in 1842 and lived during a time when women weren't supposed to do anything difficult or dangerous. But Ida's powerful demeanor challenged people's ideas about what women could do.

No Job for a Girl

When Ida was 15, she and her family moved to a lighthouse on the tiny island of Lime Rock. Her father's job was to keep the lights in the lighthouse burning so ships wouldn't crash into the island's rocky shore. Soon, though, Ida's father became sick and Ida took over his duties. She spent the rest of her life guiding sailors through the dangerous harbor. Lighthouse keeper was considered a "man's job," but Ida knew better. She kept the lighthouse in excellent shape and rowed to the mainland to pick up supplies. In those days, it wasn't proper for women to row boats. However, Ida was thought to be a better rower than many men.

Rescue!

Ida's rowing skills helped save lives. When Ida was 16, she emancipated 4 boys from a sinking boat. A few years later, 3 men almost drowned trying to save sheep that had run into the ocean. After Ida saved the men, she went back and saved the sheep! Over her lifetime, Ida saved at least 18 people from drowning.

America's Bravest Woman

Ida's rescues made her famous. Many people called her "the bravest woman in America." She wasn't just the lighthouse keeper's daughter anymore—she was a hero.

Rev Up Your Writing

Both Ku and Ida did things that no one thought they could do. Write about a time when you or someone you know surprised people with hidden talents. Use as many of the vocabulary words as possible but make sense.

Word Organizer

Copy this graphic organizer onto a separate piece of paper.

List words that are synonyms of *acrid*. Write your answers in the Synonyms box. Use some of the words in this box to describe an acrid food.

Then list words that are antonyms of *acrid*. Write your answers in the Antonyms box. Use some of the words in this box to describe a delicious food.

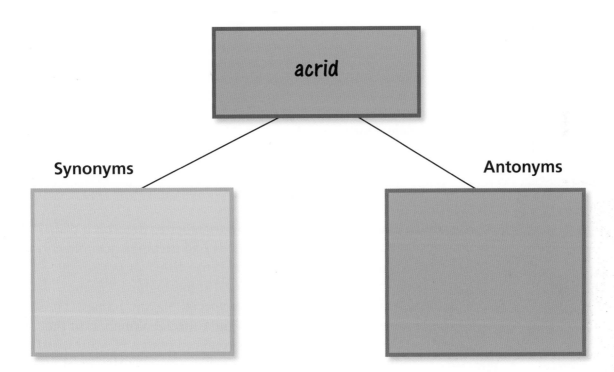

acrid

Synonyms

Antonyms

Code Talkers

Have you ever used a secret code? Maybe your friend started using a crazy code name like "Yellowjacket" for her secret crush. Codes are cool, but does anyone actually use them for anything important?

Codes have been used throughout history to keep private information from the wrong people. Even ancient Romans like Julius Caesar sent coded messages. Codes are especially important during wars. One of the most famous codes from World War II was used by people called Navajo Code Talkers.

United States soldiers wanted a code their enemies wouldn't be able to crack. In 1942, they made a fortuitous discovery. Native Americans from the Navajo tribe spoke a language that almost no one else could understand. If soldiers spoke the Navajo language, it would be hard for the enemy to figure out what they were saying.

The soldiers and the Navajos worked together to develop a code in the Navajo language. Some English words had metaphorical Navajo names. The word *submarine* was called "iron fish," or *besh-lo* in Navajo. *Fighter plane* became "hummingbird." Some words didn't have their own special Navajo names. Those words were spelled out using a special alphabet. In the alphabet, each letter was replaced with a Navajo word that started with that letter. For example, the word *ant* represented the letter *A*. The word *attack* could be spelled *ant turkey turkey ant cat kid*. All of these words were spoken in Navajo.

The United States used Navajo speakers to send coded messages during the war. The code worked almost perfectly! It's one of the only codes in history that was never cracked, and it helped the United States and its allies win World War II.

Ordinary People

Like the Navajo, other people with special skills have helped out the government in times of war.

Josephine Baker

Jazz singer Josephine Baker was the perfect person to puncture Germany's plans to take over France. Her beauty often distracted the border guards who were supposed to inspect her suitcases. When Baker crossed the border into Germany, France's plot to outwit the Germans was literally under the border guard's nose. Important secrets were written on Baker's sheet music in invisible ink!

Julia Child

During World War II, future TV chef Julia Child cooked up an acrid shark repellent for the U.S. government to paint on its underwater explosives. Before this stinky invention, sharks would run into the explosives, setting them off and informing the German Navy of which areas to avoid.

Rev Up Your Writing

Using a code can be an interesting way to communicate with someone. What's your favorite way to send messages? Do you communicate in different ways with different people? Use as many of the vocabulary words as possible but make sense.

Can You Relate?

Copy this graphic organizer onto a separate piece of paper. Match the following words with their related vocabulary word. If a word relates to more than one vocabulary word, explain why.

auspicious   Something that is auspicious will probably turn out well.
banter   If you banter with people, you tease them playfully.
loquacious   A loquacious person talks a lot.
serendipity   Serendipity is accidental or surprising good luck.
vivacious   A vivacious person is lively.

cavort	fortuitous	demeanor

In Your Own Words

VOCABULARY

acrid
puncture
literally
demeanor
cavort
emancipate
fortuitous
metaphorical
dappled
reconcile

Respond to one of the following prompts on a separate piece of paper. As you respond, use as many of the vocabulary words as possible. Be creative but make sense!

▶ Write about a time when you or someone you know worked up the courage to do something brave. Describe the sights and sounds of the experience. How did you feel? What happened afterward?

▶ Imagine you are 70 years old. Write a page from the autobiography of your life. What is your job? What is your family like? Choose one exciting event to describe in detail.

▶ Write about a topic of your choice.

The First Emperor

By Daniel Cohen

*In 1974, a Chinese farmer
accidentally discovered
an ancient buried army.
Historians and scientists believe
that this amazing find might
be just a tiny part of the greatest
hidden treasure in history.*

here is what may turn out to be the greatest archaeological find of modern times, one that may ultimately outshine even the discovery of the tomb of Tutankhamen.[1] It is the tomb of the emperor Ch'in Shih Huang Ti. Now admittedly the name Ch'in Shih Huang Ti is not exactly a household word in the West. But then neither was Tutankhamen until 1922. The major difference is that while Tutankhamen himself was historically insignificant, Ch'in Shih Huang Ti was enormously important in Chinese history. In many respects he was really the founder of China.

The future emperor started out as the king of the small state Ch'in. At the time, the land was divided up among a number of small states, all constantly warring with one another. Ch'in was one of the smallest and weakest. Yet the king of Ch'in managed to overcome all his rivals, and in the year 221 B.C. he proclaimed himself emperor of the land that we now know as China. From that date until the revolution of 1912, China was always ruled by an emperor. The name China itself comes from the name Ch'in.

Shih Huang Ti ruled his empire with ferocious efficiency. He had the Great Wall of China built to keep out the northern barbarians.[2] The Great Wall, which stretches some fifteen hundred miles, is a building project that rivals and perhaps surpasses the Great Pyramid.[3] The Great Wall took thirty years to build and cost the lives of countless thousands of laborers. Today the Great Wall remains China's number one tourist attraction.

As he grew older, Shih Huang Ti became obsessed with the prospect of his own death. He had survived several assassination[4] attempts and was terrified of another. He traveled constantly between his 270 different palaces, so that no one could ever be sure where he was going to be. He never slept in the same room for two nights in a row. Anyone who revealed the emperor's whereabouts was put to death along with his entire family.

Shih Huang Ti searched constantly for the secret of immortality. He became prey to a host[5] of phony magicians and other fakers who promised much but could deliver nothing.

FOOTNOTES

[1] *Tutankhamen:* Egyptian pharaoh whose treasure-filled tomb was discovered in 1922

[2] *barbarians:* uncivilized people

[3] *Great Pyramid:* the largest of three pyramids in Giza, Egypt

[4] *assassination:* the killing of a leader or politician

[5] *host:* a large number

The emperor heard that there were immortals living on some far-off islands, so he sent a huge fleet to find them. The commander of the fleet knew that if he failed in his mission, the emperor would put him to death. So the fleet simply never returned. It is said that the fleet found the island of Japan and stayed there to become the ancestors of the modern Japanese.

In his desire to stay alive, Shih Huang Ti did not neglect the probability[6] that he would die someday. He began construction of an immense tomb in the Black Horse hills near one of his favorite summer palaces. The tomb's construction took as long as the construction of the Great Wall—thirty years.

The emperor, of course, did die. Death came while he was visiting the eastern provinces. But his life had become so secretive that only a few high officials were aware of his death. They contrived to keep it a secret until they could consolidate their own power. The imperial procession[7] headed back for the capital. Unfortunately, it was midsummer and the emperor's body began to rot and stink. So one of the plotters arranged to have a cart of fish follow the immense imperial chariot to hide the odor of the decomposing corpse. Finally, news of the emperor's death was made public. The body, or what was left of it, was buried in the tomb that he had been building for so long.

Stories about that tomb sound absolutely incredible. It was said to contain miniature reproductions[8] of all the emperor's 270 palaces. A map of the entire empire with all the major rivers reproduced in mercury, which by some mechanical means was made to flow into a miniature ocean, was also part of the interior of the tomb. So was a reproduction of the stars and planets. According to legend, the burial chamber itself was filled with molten[9] copper so that the emperor's remains were sealed inside a gigantic ingot.[10]

It was also said that loaded crossbows were set up all around the inside of the tomb and that anyone who did manage to penetrate[11] the inner chambers would be shot full of arrows. But just to make sure that no one got that far, the pallbearers[12] who had placed Shih Huang Ti's remains in the tomb were sealed inside with it. They were supposed to be the only ones who knew exactly how to get in and out of the intricate tomb. All of this was done to preserve the emperor's remains from the hands of tomb robbers. Did it work? We don't really know yet.

FOOTNOTES

6 *probability:* the chance or likelihood
7 *procession:* a group moving together in an organized way
8 *miniature reproductions:* tiny models
9 *molten:* melted liquid
10 *ingot:* a brick of precious metal
11 *penetrate:* to break into
12 *pallbearers:* people who carry the coffin during a funeral

There are two contradictory stories about the tomb of Ch'in Shih Huang Ti. The first says that it was covered up with earth to make it resemble an ordinary hill and that its location has remained unknown for centuries.

But a more accurate legend holds that there never was any attempt to disguise the existence of the tomb. Ch'in Shih Huang Ti had been building it for years, and everybody knew where it was. After his death the tomb was surrounded by walls enclosing an area of about five hundred acres. This was to be the emperor's "spirit city." Inside the spirit city were temples and all sorts of other sacred buildings and objects dedicated to the dead emperor.

Over the centuries the walls, the temples, indeed everything above ground was carried away by vandals.[13] The top of the tomb was covered with earth and eventually came to resemble a large hill. Locally the hill is called Mount Li. But still the farmers who lived in the area had heard stories that Mount Li contained the tomb of Ch'in Shih Huang Ti or of some other important person.

In the spring of 1974 a peasant plowing a field near Mount Li uncovered a life-sized clay statue of a warrior. Further digging indicated that there was an entire army of statues beneath the ground. Though excavations[14] are not yet complete, Chinese authorities believe that there are some six thousand life-sized clay statues of warriors, plus scores of life-sized statues of horses. Most of the statues are broken, but some are in an absolutely remarkable state of preservation. Each statue is finely made, and each shows a distinct individual, different from all the others.

This incredible collection is Shih Huang Ti's "spirit army." At one time Chinese kings practiced human sacrifice so that the victims could serve the dead king in the next world. Shih Huang Ti was willing to make do with the models. Men and horses were arranged in a military fashion in a three-acre underground chamber. The chamber may have been entered at some point. The roof certainly collapsed. But still the delicate figures have survived surprisingly well. Most of the damage was done when the roof caved in. That is why the Chinese archaeologists are so hopeful that when the tomb itself is excavated, it too will be found to have survived surprisingly well.

FOOTNOTES
· · · · · · · · · · · · · · · · ·
[13] *vandals:* thieves
[14] *excavation:* the act of removing soil

The Chinese are not rushing the excavations. They have only a limited number of trained people to do the job. After all, the tomb has been there for over two thousand years. A few more years won't make much difference.

Though once denounced as a tyrant, Ch'in Shih Huang Ti is now regarded as a national hero. His name is a household word in China. The Chinese government knows that it may have an unparalleled ancient treasure on its hands, and it wants to do the job well. Over the next few years we should be hearing much more about this truly remarkable find.

Explain Yourself

Answer each question on a separate piece of paper. Be sure to explain your answers.

1. What chores would you want to do with **efficiency**? Explain.

2. How would you feel if a classmate's test score **surpassed** your own? Why?

3. Would you like to be **immortal**? Why or why not?

4. Describe a situation in which you'd **contrive** to do something.

5. How could you **consolidate** your video game collection? Explain.

6. In what ways can you help with the **preservation** of the environment?

7. How would you feel if your best friend **denounced** you? Why?

8. Would you want your text messaging skills to be **unparalleled**? Why?

9. How could you **coerce** a friend into going to a scary movie? Explain.

10. What is something that has a **fetid** smell? Explain.

efficiency If you do something with efficiency, you do it well without wasting time, money, or energy.

surpass If something surpasses something else, it is better than that thing.

immortal Someone who is immortal will live forever.

contrive When you contrive to do something, you create a plan to do it.

consolidate When you consolidate things, you bring them together.

preservation When something is in a state of preservation, it is kept from rotting or being damaged.

denounce If you denounce someone or something, you publicly speak out against it.

unparalleled Something that is unparalleled is bigger or better than everything else.

coerce If you coerce people into doing something, you pressure them to do it by threatening or intimidating them.

fetid Something that is fetid has a horrible, rotten smell.

Take It Further

Complete these sentences on a separate piece of paper.

1. Juan planned his party **efficiently** by . . .
2. Samara **surpassed** her own expectations when she . . .
3. Egyptians hoped to make the pharaoh **immortal** by . . .
4. Since her sister was busy, Juanita **contrived** to . . .
5. Jennifer **consolidated** her clothes in order to . . .
6. Many animals and insects are **preserved** when . . .
7. The protesters **denounced** the new law by . . .
8. Tamika's performance was **unparalleled** because she . . .
9. Tan **coerced** his little brother by . . .
10. The soup smelled so **fetid** that Shamika . . .

LESSON 15
DAY 4

Explore It

By now you know that if something is *fetid* it has a horrible, rotten smell. But there are also many other words that have similar meanings to the word *fetid*.

The following story contains blanks before some of the words. Number a separate piece of paper from 1-7. Using a dictionary or a thesaurus, write an adjective that can be used as a synonym for the word *fetid* next to the corresponding number on your paper.

Take it from me, whenever you have a choice of household chores, choose cleaning the _smelly_ toilet, the _____ bathtub, the _____ sink, or the _____ oven. Whatever you do, never volunteer to clean the refrigerator. I had to do it and it was the smelliest experience of my life. Until then, I never knew that two-year-old strawberry jam could turn _____, green, and grow hair! I even had to sniff the _____ old milk to see if it had turned bad. After I removed all the food, I had to wipe the shelves down with _____ vinegar. After I was done, the _____ towel smelled so bad that I had to throw it away.

PLUTO'S
Planetary Predicament

Dana Frederic spoke to Pluto, live via satellite, just hours after Pluto lost its "planethood."

Q: Thanks for chatting with me, Pluto.

P: I'd prefer to be called Pluto, Formerly Known as Planet, or PFKP. I denounce the name that these astronomers have given to me!

Q: PFKP. Sure. Please explain to our readers what has happened over the past 24 hours. How did your identity crisis begin?

PFKP: It started when a young man from Kansas named Clyde Tombaugh decided I was the mysterious Planet X that astronomers had long searched for. Clyde called me Pluto. At first, scientists thought I was much larger—maybe even as big as Earth—so calling me a planet was a no-brainer. But things changed. As telescopes got stronger, astronomers noticed that I was different. I'm smaller than my "siblings." I move very slowly in a broad orbit around the sun. Soon, astronomers weren't so sure what I was. Was I one of Neptune's moons? Was I a comet? They didn't know!

PFKP: Then an astronomy professor named Mike Brown spotted a bright object in space, in a consolidated ring of asteroids called the Kuiper Belt. Mike called it Eris.

Q: How did Eris make trouble for you?

PFKP: Finding Eris got people asking: Is Eris a planet? How many other planets exist?

Q: Why do you think the International Astronomical Union (IAU) took the unparalleled step of kicking you out of the planet club?

PFKP: I think they were coerced by the discoveries of new space objects that were similar to me. Some scientists thought I was just hitching a ride off Neptune. But that wasn't the worst . . . When they declared I was probably just another piece of space rock like the ones in the asteroid belt between Mars and Jupiter, I hit a new low. Now there are only eight planets in the solar system, and I'm not one of them.

Q: Astounding! How does that make you feel?

PFKP: How do you think I feel? I feel like the ugly duckling! Who wants to wake up one day to find out that you aren't who you thought you were?

Q: There you have it. I guess science's immortal quest for knowledge can bring about huge changes and lost souls.

Rev Up Your Writing

You've just read about Pluto's recent name change. Now write about how you would feel if someone asked you to change your name. Use as many of the vocabulary words as possible but make sense.

Word Organizer

Copy this graphic organizer onto a separate piece of paper.

Coerce is near the hot end of the Word-O-Meter. Think of words that would be colder than *coerce*. Write your answers in the boxes. Explain your answers.

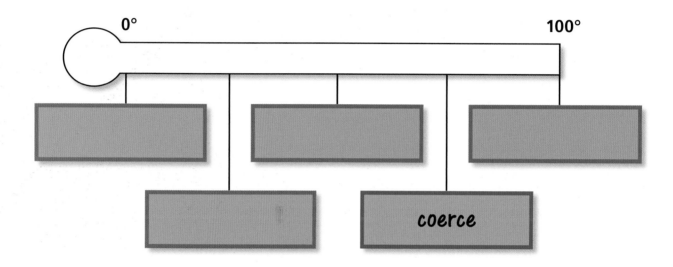

0°   100°

coerce

"What has been the effect of
coercion? To make one-half of the world
fools and the other half hypocrites."
–Thomas Jefferson

Strange Snake Tales

Two-Headed Snake Learns to Share

PINOSO, Spain—Two-headed ladder snake is lucky to be alive.

You might think having two heads would make you a more efficient eater. Wrong! The heads get in the way for most animals. For this little snake, having two heads is deadly. Its heads often fight over who eats first. When one head has a mouse, the other head smells the mouse and tries to swallow the first head!

Old Man Survives 272 Snakebites

NEW DELHI, India—Man claims to have survived 272 snakebites. He credits his luck to following a healer's tip: Don't eat salt!

Ninety-two-year-old Amar Singh says he loves snakes even though he has been bitten many times.

Singh learned his survival tip more than 50 years ago. Most others who have tried Singh's tip have not survived to tell their tales.

Teen Lives to Celebrate Birthday

Florida, USA—After almost dying from a snakebite, a teen celebrates his birthday.

Thirteen-year-old Mikey Evans knew the second he felt a sting that a snake had bitten him. Instead of thinking of his own preservation, the brave teen lifted his ten-year-old friend onto his back. Then he carried his friend to safety, 70 feet away.

Rescuers would later find out that Mikey was bitten not once, but four times. It turns out the teen stepped into a rattlesnake's nest.

Yellow Albino Burmese Pythons are not venomous. They wrap their bodies around their prey and squeeze them to death.

Robbers Bite Off More Than They Can Chew

SYDNEY, Australia—Unlucky thieves beware! One of the four snakes recently stolen from a wildlife park is deadly.

The thieves probably contrived to nab a sack full of harmless water snakes. But this gang is in for a big surprise! The Collett's snake is the 18th most deadly in the world. One bite from the unusual loot could cost the thieves their lives.

Need Snakebite Cure? Don't Look to the Movies

Tennessee, USA—Snakebite survivor Mike Edwards shares his lesson learned: Don't take medical advice from a movie.

While waiting for rescuers to arrive, 46-year-old Edwards was helped by a stranger who must have seen too many Western movies. The woman tied a tourniquet, or tight bandage, around Mike's arm, as she'd seen on the big screen. Instead of helping, she made it worse. The tourniquet kept the venom in Mike's arm. The trapped poison attacked his flesh. Mike could have lost his hand if the fetid poison was trapped there for too long. Fortunately, medics removed the bandage in time to save Mike's arm.

Snake Wraps Self Around Boy, Then Bites

VICTORIA, Australia—A snake wrapped itself around a thirteen-year-old schoolboy's leg. Then it sank its fangs into his shin! The snake's anger surpassed all expectations.

The 3-foot-long brown snake slithered into the grass when the boy cried for help. Teachers kept him calm so that the venom would not spread. After a trip to the hospital he is doing well.

Rev Up Your Writing

These snakebite survivors all have one thing in common—luck. Write about a time you or someone you know escaped a dangerous situation. Use as many of the vocabulary words as possible but make sense.

Can You Relate?

Copy this graphic organizer onto a separate piece of paper. Match the following words with their related vocabulary word. If a word relates to more than one word, explain why.

colossal   If something is colossal, it is very large.
enduring   When something is enduring, it is long lasting.
perennial   If something is perennial, it is everlasting.
transcend   When something transcends normal limits, it moves beyond them.
ultimate   If something is the ultimate, it is the best possible.

surpass	immortal	unparalleled

LESSON 15

DAY
9

In Your Own Words

Respond to one of the following prompts on a separate piece of paper. As you respond, use as many of the vocabulary words as possible. Be creative but make sense!

▶ Write about something amazing or frightening that you or someone you know has seen or experienced. Use descriptive words that will convey just how amazing or frightening it was.

▶ Write a letter to the editor of your local paper about how Pluto has been treated. Explain why you think the decision to rename it was fair or unfair.

▶ Write about a topic of your choice.

VOCABULARY

efficiency
surpass
immortal
contrive
consolidate
preservation
denounce
unparalleled
coerce
fetid

189

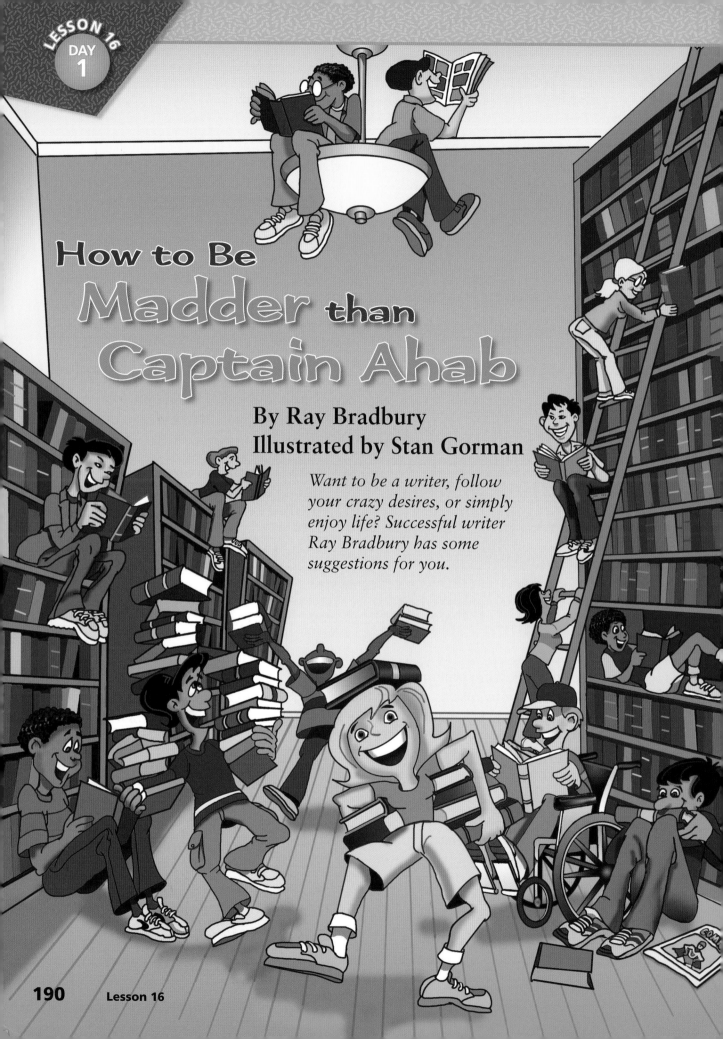

How to Be Madder than Captain Ahab

By Ray Bradbury
Illustrated by Stan Gorman

Want to be a writer, follow your crazy desires, or simply enjoy life? Successful writer Ray Bradbury has some suggestions for you.

How does one go about becoming a writer?

Well, you might as well ask, how do you go about becoming human, whatever *that* is!

I suppose you fall in love, early, with all kinds of things.

I fell in love with books when I was five or six, especially the way books looked and smelled.

I have been a library jackdaw[1] all of my life, which means I have never gone into that lovely holy place with a book list, but only with my beady bright eyes and my curious paws, monkey-climbing the stacks over among the children's, and then again where I was not allowed, burrowing among the adult's mysterious books.

I would take home, at the age of ten, eight books at a time, from eight different categories, and rub my nose in them and all but lie down and roll on them like a frolicsome springtime dog. *Popular Mechanics* and *The Boy Mechanic* were my bibles. The encyclopedia was my open meadow-field where I rambled and muttered: "curiouser and curiouser!" and lay down with Jules Verne's robot pups only to arise with Edgar Rice Burroughs' Martian fleas.

I have run amuck[2] ever since in libraries and bookstores, with fevers and deliriums.

Hysteria[3] must be your way of life, then, if you wish, any of you, to become writers. Or, for that matter, painters or actors or any other crazy, lovely things!

If I emphasize libraries it is because school itself is only a beginning and writing itself is a continuation. But the meat must be found and fed on[4] in every library you can jump into and every bookstore you can pole-vault through.

Even as I did not prowl there with preconceived lists, so I do not send you there with nice dry tame indexes of my taste crushing you with an iron anvil dropped from a building.

Once started, the library is the biggest blasted Cracker Jack[5] factory in the world.

The more you eat, the more you want!

FOOTNOTES
1 *jackdaw:* a type of bird
2 *amuck:* wildly
3 *Hysteria:* panic, excitement
4 *But the meat must be found and fed on:* good books must be found and read
5 *Cracker Jack:* a sweet popcorn snack

And the more you read, the more the ideas begin to explode around inside your head, run riot, meet head-on in beautiful collisions so that when you go to bed at night the . . . visions color the ceiling and light the walls with huge exploits and wonderful discoveries.

I still use libraries and bookstores in the same fashion, forty years later. I spend as much time in child's country[6] as I do over the corseted adults'.[7]

And what I take home and browse and munch through each evening should give you a relaxing view of a writer tumultuous just this side of madness.

I may start a night's read with a James Bond novel, move on to Shakespeare for half an hour, dip into Dylan Thomas for five minutes, make a fast turnabout and fasten on Fu Manchu, that great and evil Oriental doctor, ancestor of Dr. No, then pick up Emily Dickinson, and end my evening with Ross MacDonald, the detective novelist, or Robert Frost, that crusty poet of the American rural spirit.

The fact should be plain now: I am an amiable compost heap. My mind is full of moron plus brilliant trash, shoved in my eyes and sticking out of my ears and elbows. For I learned early on, that in order to grow myself excellent, I had to start myself in plain old farmyard blood manure. From such heaps of mediocre or angelic words, I fever myself up to grow fine stories, or roses, if you prefer.

I am a junkyard, then, of all the libraries and bookstores I ever fell into or leaned upon, and am proud that I never developed such a rare taste that I could not go back and jog with Tarzan or hit the Yellow Brick Road with Dorothy, both characters and their books banned for fifty years by all librarians and most educators. I have had my own loves, and gone my own way to become my own self.

I highly recommend you do the same. However crazy your desire, however wild your need, however dumb your taste may seem to others . . . follow it!

When I was nine, I collected Buck Rogers comic strips. People made fun. I tore them up. Two months later, I said to myself: "Hold on! What's this all about? These people are trying to starve me. They have cut me off from my vitamins! And the greatest food in my life, right now, is Buck Rogers! Everyone, outa the way! Git! Runty Ray is going to start collecting comic strips again!"

And I did. For I have the great secret!

Everyone else was wrong. I was right. For me anyway.

What if I hadn't done as I have done?

Would I ever have grown up to become a writer of science fictions or, for that matter, any kind of writer at all?

No. Never.

If I had listened to all taste-mongers and fools and critics, I would have played a safe game, never jumped the fence,[8] and become a nonentity whose name would not be known to you now.

So it was I learned to run and leap into an empty swimming pool, hoping to sweat enough liquid into it on the way down to make a soft landing.

Or, to change metaphors, I dropped myself off the edges of cliffs, daring to build myself wings while falling, so as not to break myself on the rocks below.

To sum it all up, if you want to write, if you want to create, you must be the most sublime fool that God ever turned out and sent rambling.

You must write every single day of your life.

You must read dreadful dumb books and glorious books, and let them wrestle in beautiful fights inside your head, vulgar one moment, brilliant the next.

You must lurk in libraries and climb the stacks like ladders to snuff books like perfumes and wear books like hats upon your crazy heads.

I wish for you a wrestling match with your Creative Muse[9] that will last a lifetime.

I wish craziness and foolishness and madness upon you.

May you live with hysteria, and out of it make fine stories.

Which finally means, may you be in love every day for the next 20,000 days. And out of the love, remake a world.

Explain Yourself

VOCABULARY

Answer each question on a separate piece of paper. Be sure to explain your answers.

1. Are you usually **frolicsome** before you go to bed? Why or why not?

2. Would you experience **delirium** if you won a million dollars? Explain.

3. Would you want people to have **preconceived** ideas about you? Why or why not?

4. What **exploit** would you most like to experience? Explain.

5. Would you want your school to be a **tumultuous** place? Why or why not?

6. Would you recommend a **sublime** book to a friend? Explain.

7. Why might your dog **lurk** in the kitchen?

8. What kinds of things might be in an **eclectic** lunch? Explain.

9. What would you really like to **immerse** yourself in? Why?

10. What subject or activity are you **zealous** about? Explain.

frolicsome   Someone who is frolicsome is very playful and energetic.

delirium   If you experience delirium, you're confused and crazed because you are really sick or excited.

preconceived   If you have preconceived ideas, you've made up your mind before you have enough information.

exploit   An exploit is a brave and daring adventure.

tumultuous   If something is tumultuous, it is wild and out of control.

sublime   If something is sublime, it is wonderful and awe inspiring.

lurk   Someone who is lurking somewhere is waiting around and doesn't want to be seen.

eclectic   Something that is eclectic is made up of a wide variety of things.

immerse   When you immerse yourself in something, you completely surround yourself with it.

zealous   If you are zealous, you are extremely enthusiastic about a particular activity or belief.

Take It Further

Complete these sentences on a separate piece of paper.

1. A **frolicsome** child might . . .

2. Clive experienced **delirium** when he . . .

3. Greta's ideas about rap music were **preconceived** because . . .

4. Anita's **exploits** included . . .

5. The crowd became **tumultuous** when . . .

6. Victor thought the play was **sublime** because . . .

7. Lily and Rosa were **lurking** in the backyard because . . .

8. Earl had an **eclectic** . . .

9. Lance was **immersed** in music when he . . .

10. We could tell Cherice was **zealous** about . . .

Explore It

Since you know that having a preconceived idea means that you formed your idea in advance, you can probably tell that the prefix *pre–* means "before" or "in advance."

Working with someone else, unscramble the words using the clues provided. Write your answers down on your own piece of paper and be ready to explain yourself!

1. Take a sneak peek!   pre _ _ _ _ (ewiv)

2. Mom bought the movie tickets on the Internet and picked them up at the theater.   pre_ _ _ _ (idpa)

3. You may need to do this if you want to get that grape juice stain out of your T-shirt.   pre _ _ _ _ (kaos)

4. Warm up the oven before you bake that pie!   pre _ _ _ _ (aeth)

5. I went to a special program that got me ready for Kindergarten.   pre _ _ _ _ _ _ (osohlc)

How'd They Do That?

LIQUID LATEX

FACIAL PAINT

Before

By now, you've probably realized that the gory characters in your favorite sci-fi or action movie are really fine works of art—special effects make-up art, that is. Special effects make-up is an eclectic mix of chemicals, foam, specially made rubber and plastic pieces, and other materials. It takes a team of highly skilled make-up artists to use these materials to transform an actor into a totally new character.

These zealous makeup artists may spend many weeks sketching images, making artificial replacement pieces, and blending just the right colors and textures to make their preconceived ideas a reality. Before a character is put into full costume, the materials are tested. Actors and actresses participate in these tests to be sure that the materials will not cause any allergic reactions.

When it's time to have their makeup applied, the actors must sit or lie still for hours while a team of make-up artists poke, spray, pour, pull, press, paint, and rub things all over them. After their appearance has been transformed, the actors may have to sit perfectly still for a few more hours until the director is ready to begin filming for that day.

The next time you watch a DVD and see characters wearing crazy makeup, check out the bonus features to see if there's a clip showing how the actors were transformed into their characters. What you learn may surprise you. It may even inspire you to immerse yourself in the study of special effects make-up. Who knows—maybe you'll become a sublime special effects make-up artist!

Try It!

Want to try your own special effects make-up? Follow these easy steps to give yourself instant wrinkles!

① **BLOW OUT** your cheeks as big as you can. Continue breathing through your nose.

② **APPLY** a layer of liquid latex* with a sponge. (*Caution: liquid latex can cause a rash.)

③ **LET IT DRY.** A hairdryer can speed the drying process, but be careful not to burn yourself!

④ Let your **CHEEKS** relax and check out your wrinkles!

Bonus: for an extra-elderly look, sprinkle some baby powder in your hair!

After

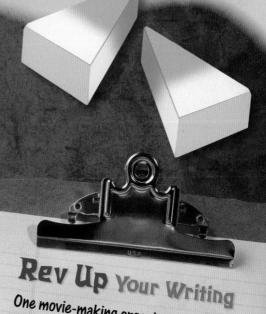

Rev Up Your Writing

One movie-making organization wants to stop including special effects in movies. Write a letter to the organization explaining why they should or should not do this. Be sure to include examples of good (or bad) special effects to support your opinion. Use as many of the vocabulary words as possible but make sense.

Word Organizer

Copy this graphic organizer onto a separate piece of paper.

List words that mean almost the same thing as *delirium* and write your answers in the web.

Then tell about a time when you experienced delirium.

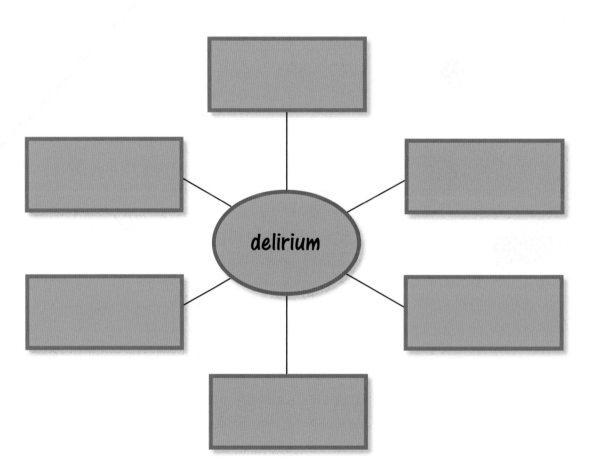

THE ORIGINAL MIME

A MYTH

Montgomery Mimel was quite the adventurer. Every summer he sailed around the globe to explore unknown lands. When he returned, he always had fascinating tales to share. Once he dined with the sharks in the Pacific. Another time he swam with a frolicsome dolphin in the Atlantic. He even outran the cheetahs in the sub-Saharan desert to get the best spot for an afternoon nap.

One summer he decided to journey to the African savannah. He wanted to climb atop an elephant to get a better view of the area. After docking his boat and walking for miles and miles in the hot sun, he spotted a huge African elephant grazing with its herd. Montgomery hoped the elephant would not see him lurking in the bushes. He was hoping to climb aboard the elephant while it wasn't looking.

When the time was right, Montgomery ran toward the elephant as fast as he could. Just when he was about to jump onto the elephant's back, one of the other elephants nearby noticed him and trumpeted a warning. His elephant moved quickly, and Montgomery fell flat on his back. The elephant must have thought he was dangerous, so it took off running, stepping on Montgomery's hand on the way by. He had never felt such intense pain! He let out a thunderous cry. He had never yelled so loudly before. He yelled so loudly that he felt like his voice was leaving his body forever. Even worse, he yelled so loudly that he started a tumultuous stampede!

In a state of delirium, Montgomery jumped up and ran as fast as he could back to his boat. Once he was safely afloat, he cradled his aching hand and tried to rest his sore throat while he thought about the great story he had to share with his friends.

When everyone gathered around the fire to hear about Montgomery's exploits, something strange happened. He opened his mouth to talk, but no words came out. He tried again, but his loud yelling must have permanently damaged his vocal chords. He tried and tried to tell what had happened, but everyone just laughed at him as he waved his arms and made funny faces.

For the remainder of his life, Montgomery could be found in the town square still trying to tell his story. He used his hands, face, and body to try to talk to people, but nothing seemed to work. He even painted his face white because he thought it would help people understand his facial expressions better. Most of the time, people just laughed at him.

The memory of Montgomery Mimel still lives on. Though he's been dead for hundreds of years, people in many countries around the world paint their faces white and stand in town squares to tell his story with gestures. You may know these people as "mimes."

Rev Up Your Writing

You've just read about an adventurer who traveled around the world. If you could travel anywhere in the world, where would you go and why? What would you want to explore there? Use as many of the vocabulary words as possible but make sense.

Can You Relate?

Copy this graphic organizer onto a separate piece of paper. Match the following words with their related vocabulary word. If a word relates to more than one vocabulary word, explain why.

avid   Avid people are very enthusiastic about particular activities.
ebullient   When someone is ebullient, he or she is very lively and cheerful.
gambol   If you gambol, you run around playfully.
garner   If you garner things, you gather or collect them.
motley   A motley collection contains a wide variety of different things.

frolicsome	zealous	eclectic

In Your Own Words

Respond to one of the following prompts on a separate piece of paper. As you respond, use as many of the vocabulary words as possible. Be creative but make sense!

▶ Write about a time when you or someone you know performed in front of an audience. What was the performance? How did you feel before the performance? Did you feel different afterward?

▶ Write a funny essay about your favorite activity. Use silly images and crazy comparisons to make your essay come to life.

▶ Write about a topic of your choice.

VOCABULARY

frolicsome
delirium
preconceived
exploit
tumultuous
sublime
lurk
eclectic
immerse
zealous

Glossary

A

abyss (uh BIHS) An abyss is a hole or space so big and deep that it seems bottomless.

accordingly (uh KAWR dihng lee) When you do something accordingly, you do it as a result of something else.

accumulate (uh KYOO myuh layt) When you accumulate things, you gather or collect them over time.

acrid (AK rihd) An acrid smell or taste is unpleasantly strong and bitter.

acute (uh KYOOT) If something is acute, it is sensitive and powerful enough to detect even the smallest change.

adept (uh DEHPT) Someone who is adept is very good at doing something.

adroit (uh DROYT) If you are adroit, you are skillful and clever, especially in difficult situations.

affluent (AF lu uhnt) Affluent people have a lot of money.

anecdote (AN ihk doht) An anecdote is a short, entertaining story about something that has happened.

appalling (uh PAW lihng) Something that is appalling is horrifying, shocking, or frightening.

appraise (uh PRAYZ) When you appraise something, you decide how valuable you think it is.

arrogant (AR uh guhnt) Arrogant people think they are better than everyone else.

aversion (uh VUR zhuhn) If you have an aversion to something, you really don't like it.

B

barren (BAR uhn) A barren place is empty, dry, or unable to grow things.

benevolent (buh NEHV uh luhnt) Benevolent people are kind and patient.

boisterous (BOYS tuhr uhs) Someone or something that is boisterous is noisy and excited.

bolster (BOHL stuhr) If you bolster something, you support it and make it stronger.

brunt (bruhnt) If you experience the brunt of something, you get the full force or worst part of it.

buffet (BUHF iht) If something buffets something else, it hits or pushes it violently and repeatedly.

C

cavort (kuh VAWRT) Someone or something that cavorts leaps about in a playful and excited way.

clandestine (klan DEHS tuhn) A clandestine act is done in secret, probably because it is wrong or illegal.

coerce (koh URS) If you coerce people into doing something, you pressure them to do it by threatening or intimidating them.

combustible (kuhm BUHS tuh buhl) If something is combustible, you can burn it easily.

concoct (kon KOKT) If you concoct something, you make it up on the spot by putting several things together.

condemn (kuhn DEHM) If someone is condemned, he or she is thought to be guilty and is punished.

conform (kuhn FAWRM) If you conform, you make yourself the same as everyone else.

confound (kuhn FOWND) If something confounds you, it confuses you.

consent (kuhn SEHNT) When you consent to something, you agree to do it or to let it be done.

consolidate (kuhn SOL uh dayt) When you consolidate things, you bring them together.

conspire (kuhn SPYR) When people conspire to do something, they secretly plan to do it.

consternation (KON stuhr NAY shuhn) Consternation is a feeling of nervousness or alarm.

contrive (kuhn TRYV) When you contrive to do something, you create a plan to do it.

conundrum (kuh NUHN druhm) A conundrum is a mystery, puzzle, or problem.

copious (KOH pee uhs) If you have a copious amount of something, you have a lot of it.

crescendo (kruh SHEHN doh) A crescendo is a sound that gets louder and louder.

cultivate (KUHL tuh vayt) If you cultivate something, you take care of it and try to make it grow.

D

dappled (DAP uhld) Something that is dappled has a lot of spots on it.

dearth (durth) When there is a dearth of something, there is not enough of it.

debilitate (dih BIHL uh tayt) If a problem debilitates you, it weakens you so that you are unable to live your life in a normal way.

decipher (dih SY fuhr) If you decipher something, you figure out something that is difficult to understand.

delirium (dih LIHR ee uhm) If you experience delirium, you're confused and crazed because you are really sick or excited.

deluge (DEHL yooj) A deluge is a large amount of something coming at you all at once, such as a heavy rainstorm.

demeanor (dih MEE nuhr) Your demeanor is your appearance or behavior.

denounce (dih NOWNS) If you denounce someone or something, you publicly speak out against it.

deride (dih RYD) If you deride someone or something, you laugh at it and make fun of it.

despair (dih SPAIR) When you despair, you feel like there is no hope.

destitute (DEHS tuh toot) A destitute person is extremely poor.

devastation (DEHV uh STAY shuhn) Devastation is total, widespread destruction.

deviate (DEE vee ayt) If you deviate from something, you go a different direction or do things differently than was planned.

devise (dih VYZ) When you devise a way to do something, you invent a creative way of doing it.

dictate (DIHK tayt) A dictate is a rule you have to follow.

dire (dyr) If a situation is dire, it is extremely bad and it seems like there is no hope.

discard (dihs KAHRD) When you discard something, you throw it away or get rid of it.

discreet (dihs KREET) When people are discreet, they behave in a way that does not draw attention to themselves.

disdainful (dihs DAYN fuhl) If you are disdainful, you look down on others because you believe you are better.

disillusioned (DIHS ih LOO zhuhnd) If you are disillusioned, you realize that something or someone is not as good as you thought.

disperse (dihs PURS) When something disperses, it breaks apart and scatters in different directions.

docile (DOS uhl) Someone or something that is docile is calm and easy to control.

E

eclectic (ehk LEHK tihk) Something that is eclectic is made up of a wide variety of things.

eclipse (ih KLIHPS) If something eclipses something else, it takes the attention away from it by being larger or more important.

ecstatic (ehk STAT ihk) If you are ecstatic, you are extremely happy and excited.

efficiency (uh FIHSH uhn see) If you do something with efficiency, you do it well without wasting time, money, or energy.

emancipate (ih MAN suh payt) When you emancipate someone or something, you set it free.

emblazon (ehm BLAY zuhn) When you emblazon something, you display it in a very noticeable way.

entice (ehn TYS) If you entice someone to do something, you get him or her to do it by making it seem appealing.

erratic (uh RAT ihk) Something erratic happens in odd, unpredictable patterns.

eternal (ih TUR nuhl) Something that is eternal has no beginning and no end.

expectant (ehk SPEHK tuhnt) When you are expectant, you think something is about to happen.

exploit (EHKS ployt) An exploit is a brave and daring adventure.

F

fetid (FEHT ihd) Something that is fetid has a horrible, rotten smell.

flourish (FLUR ihsh) If something flourishes, it is healthy, strong, and successful.

fortitude (FAWR tuh tood) A person who has fortitude faces danger or pain with calm bravery.

fortuitous (fawr TOO uh tuhs) You say it is fortuitous when something good happens just by chance.

frolicsome (FROL ihk suhm) Someone who is frolicsome is very playful and energetic.

G

glut (gluht) If you are glutted with something, you have so much of it you can never use it all.

grace (grays) Grace is a smooth, elegant way of doing something.

guise (gyz) A guise is a false appearance.

H

harness (HAHR nihs) When you harness something, you take control of it and direct how it is used.

I

immerse (ih MURS) When you immerse yourself in something, you completely surround yourself with it.

immortal (ih MAWR tuhl) Someone who is immortal will live forever.

impede (ihm PEED) If something impedes you, it gets in your way or makes things more difficult for you.

impending (ihm PEHN dihng) If something is impending, there are signs that it is about to happen.

impose (ihm POHZ) When you impose something on people, you force it on them.

imprudent (ihm PROO duhnt) When you do something imprudent, you act without thinking through the consequences.

inadvertently (IHN uhd VUR tuhnt lee) If you do something inadvertently, you do it accidentally.

inaugurate (ihn AW gyuh rayt) When you inaugurate something, you officially begin it.

incensed (ihn SEHNSD) If you are incensed about something, you are extremely angry and insulted by it.

incoherent (IHN koh HIHR uhnt) If someone or something is incoherent, it is not clear and is difficult to understand.

inconclusive (IHN kuhn KLOO sihv) If something is inconclusive, it does not prove anything or comes to no conclusion.

incorporate (ihn KAWR puh rayt) If you incorporate things, you include them or bring them together.

incur (ihn KUR) When you incur something unpleasant, it happens because of something you did.

indignant (ihn DIHG nuhnt) If you are indignant, you are angry about something that seems unfair.

insatiable (ihn SAY shuh buhl) Someone who is insatiable can't get enough and is never satisfied.

insolent (IHN suh luhnt) An insolent person is rude and disrespectful.

intact (ihn TAKT) If something is intact, it is whole and has not been damaged.

interminable (ihn TUR muh nuh buhl) If something is interminable, it seems like it's taking forever.

intrepid (ihn TREHP ihd) An intrepid person is brave and determined and doesn't let obstacles get in the way.

intrigue (ihn TREEG) When someone or something intrigues you, it fascinates you and makes you curious.

ironic (y RON ihk) If something is ironic, it is strange or funny because it is the opposite of what you would expect.

irrevocable (ih REHV uh kuh buhl) An action that is irrevocable cannot be undone or revoked.

J

jubilant (JOO buh luhnt) Someone who is jubilant feels great joy and excitement.

L

laden (LAY duhn) If someone or something is laden, it is carrying heavy things or burdens.

languish (LANG gwihsh) When you languish through something, you suffer and become weak.

literally (LIHT uhr uh lee) If something is said to have literally happened, it actually happened the way it was described.

looming (LOOM ihng) If something is looming over you, it feels like a big and frightening problem.

lucid (LOO sihd) Something lucid is plain and clear or easy to understand.

lurk (lurk) Someone who is lurking somewhere is waiting around and doesn't want to be seen.

M

magnanimous (mag NAN uh muhs) A magnanimous person is very generous.

maw (maw) A maw is the mouth or jaws of a vicious animal.

meritorious (MEHR uh TOHR ee uhs) Someone or something that is meritorious deserves praise and honor.

metaphorical (MEHT uh FOR uh kuhl) You are being metaphorical when you describe something by using images or symbols.

miserly (MY zuhr lee) A miserly person is stingy and doesn't want to give away anything.

musty (MUHS tee) Something that is musty smells damp and old.

N

noxious (NOK shuhs) A noxious substance will damage your health and may kill you.

O

obstinate (OB stuh niht) If you are obstinate, you are stubborn.

P

peripheral (puh RIHF uhr uhl) Something that is described as being peripheral to something else is on the outer part of it.

plod (plod) Someone who plods walks slowly and heavily, without much energy or excitement.

ponderous (PON duhr uhs) Something ponderous is heavy and slow moving.

portent (POHR tehnt) A portent is a warning sign that something bad is about to happen.

preconceived (PREE kuhn SEEVD) If you have preconceived ideas, you've made up your mind before you have enough information.

prerogative (prih ROG uh tihv) If you say that something is your prerogative, you claim the right or privilege to do it.

preservation (PREHZ uhr VAY shuhn) When something is in a state of preservation, it is kept from rotting or being damaged.

puncture (PUHNGK chuhr) If you puncture something, you make a small hole in it.

R

ramification (RAM uh fuh KAY shuhn) If some action has ramifications, there are possible consequences that you might not have thought of.

rashly (rash lee) If you act rashly, you act too quickly and without thinking.

realm (rehlm) A realm is an area under someone or something's control.

reconcile (REHK uhn syl) If you reconcile yourself to a situation, you accept it as it is.

remorse (rih MAWRS) If you feel remorse about something you did, you feel guilt and regret.

repentance (rih PEHN tuhns) Repentance is a feeling of sorrow and regret for something you did that was wrong.

retract (rih TRAKT) If something retracts, it pulls back or in.

reverie (REHV uhr ee) A reverie is a long daydream full of pleasant thoughts.

revitalize (ree VY tuh lyz) When you are revitalized, you feel as though you have been given new life and energy.

revive (rih VYV) If you revive someone or something, you give it new life or new energy.

S

sagacious (suh GEI shuhs) Someone who is sagacious is wise and gives good advice.

shun (shuhn) If you shun something, you stay away from it because you don't want to be involved with it.

sinister (SIHN uh stuhr) Something sinister is evil looking and scary.

slighted (SLY tehd) If you feel slighted, you feel left out or looked down upon.

snide (snyd) Someone who is snide is rude in a sneaky way.

solemnly (SOL uhm lee) When you do something solemnly, you do it in a very serious, almost sad way.

solicit (suh LIHS iht) When you solicit something, you ask someone for it.

stench (stehnch) If something has a stench, it has a very terrible smell.

stout (stowt) Someone or something that is stout is strong, thick, and heavy for its size.

sublime (suh BLYM) If something is sublime, it is wonderful and awe inspiring.

submerge (suhb MURJ) Something that is submerged is completely covered by a liquid.

surpass (suhr PAS) If something surpasses something else, it is better than that thing.

T

tangible (TAN juh buhl) Something that is tangible can be touched.

tawdry (TAW dree) Something tawdry is cheap looking and usually in bad taste.

trigger (TRIHG uhr) If something triggers an event, it makes the event happen.

tumultuous (too MUHL chu uhs) If something is tumultuous, it is wild and out of control.

turbulence (TUR byuh luhns) Turbulence is a disturbance that is caused by wild, unpredictable, and constantly changing conditions.

U

unceremoniously (UHN sehr uh MOH nee uhs lee) If you do something unceremoniously, you do it quickly and without manners.

unconsciously (uhn KON shuhs lee) If you do something unconsciously, you do it without being aware that you are doing it.

unconventional (UHN kuhn VEHN shuh nuhl) Someone or something that is unconventional is different from the usual.

undaunted (uhn DAWN tihd) If you are undaunted, you aren't worried or discouraged by things that happen.

unfetter (uhn FEHT uhr) When you unfetter something, you free it.

unparalleled (uhn PAR uh lehld) Something that is unparalleled is bigger or better than everything else.

unsettling (uhn SEHT lihng) Something unsettling makes you feel uneasy or disturbed.

W

wallow (WOL oh) If you wallow through something, you move through it slowly and with difficulty.

waver (WAY vuhr) When someone or something wavers, it moves back and forth or cannot make a decision.

Z

zealous (ZEHL uhs) If you are zealous, you are extremely enthusiastic about a particular activity or belief.

Acknowledgments

Grateful acknowledgment is given to the following sources for illustrations and photography:

Illustration

P.19 Brie Spangler; pp.21-23 Valerie Sokolova; pp.27, 29 Harry Briggs; p.42 David Tamura; p.53 Richard Stergulz; pp.80-81, 84 Cynthia Watts Clark; p.87 Nancy Harrison; p.88 Judy DuFour Love; p.97 Kim Johnson-Husu; p.98 Jared Osterrhold; p.100 Nancy Harrison; pp.103-104, 106 Olwyn Whelan; p.109 Aaron Jasinski; p.112 Roger Roth; pp.115-116, 118 Winson Trang; pp.127-128, 131 Twila Schofield; p.135 Carlos Castellanos; p.147 Shayne Letain; p.148 Chris Walker; p.150 Brian Dow; p.162 William Ersland; pp.165-166, 168 Meryl Treatner; p.171 Margaret Ringia Hart; p.190 Stan Gorman; p.196 Jeff Grunewald; p.200 Hrana Janto.

Photography

P.8 ©iStockphoto; p.9 ©Royalty Free/CORBIS; p.12 ©Bettmann/Corbis; p.15b ©Weatherstock/ Warren Faidley Rights Managed; p.16c ©Photodisc Red/Getty Images; p.18a ©Sean Justice/Corbis; p.18c ©Jeff Greenberg/Photo Edit; p.29a ©Digital Vision/Getty Images; p.32 ©Benjamin Lowry/Corbis; p.33 ©SuperStock; p.35 ©Steve Vidler/SuperStock; p.38a ©Don Farrall/Getty Images; p.39a ©Katrina Brown/Shutterstock; p.39b ©"House of Wax" Vincent Price, Phyllix Kirk 1953 Warner Brothers ** I.V.; p.44 Steve Bly/Alamy; p.45 ©Getty Royalty Free; p.46 ©Steve Bly/Alamy Royalty Free; p.49 ©George S de Blonsky/Alamy; p.50b ©Powl Pictures/ zefa/Corbis; p.50c ©Milhail Voskresensky/Reuters/ Corbis; p.52d ©2007 Jupiterimages Corporation; p.55 ©Dwight Carter; p.58 ©Bettmann/CORBIS; p.61a ©Fotosearch; p.61b ©iStockphoto; p.61c ©Bettmann/CORBIS; p.62a ©Bettmann/CORBIS; p.62b ©Ted Thai/Getty Images; p.62c ©Bettmann/ CORBIS; pp.64-65 ©Harrod Blank www. artcarworld.org; p.67a ©AP Photo/West Hawaii Today, Michael Darden; p.67b ©Joe Patronite/ Stringer/Getty Images; pp.68-69 ©John F. White/ SuperStock; pp.70-71 ©age fotostock/SuperStock; p.74a ©Bettmann/Corbis; p.74b ©Underwood Photo Archives/SuperStock; p.75 ©SuperStock, Inc./SuperStock; p.90a ©Philip Gould/CORBIS; p.91a ©Thomas Goskar; p.91b ©Paul Seheult/Eye Ubiquitous/Corbis; pp.93, 94a ©Pixoi Ltd./Alamy; p.94b ©Tony Charnock/Alamy; p.101a ©Dag Sundberg/The Image Bank/Getty Images; p.113a ©GK Hart/Vikki Hart/Photographer's Choice/Getty Images; p.124a ©Jaimie Duplass/Shutterstock; p.124b ©George Doyle & Ciaran Griffin/Stockdisc Classic/Getty Images; p.134e ©Vladimir V. Georgievskiy/Shutterstock; p.134f ©Billy Lobo H./ Shutterstock; p.135b ©Billy Lobo H./Shutterstock; p.137 ©Keren Su/China Span/Alamy; p.138c ©CORBIS; p.138d ©Arnie Hodalic of Slovenia; p.140 ©Popperfoto/Alamy; p.141 ©Richard List/ CORBIS; p.144 ©Popperfoto/Alamy; p.151b ©Matt Knannlein/iStockphoto; p.151d ©Ralph Juergen Kraft/Shutterstock; p.153 Courtesy of the Library of Congress; pp.154, 156 ©Bettmann/CORBIS; p.159a ©Nancy Kaszerman/ZUMA/Corbis; p.159b ©Ana Blazic/iStockPhoto; p.160 ©2007 Masterfile Corporation; p.172b ©Jeremy D'Entremont; p.172c ©USCG Historians Office; p.174a ©Bettmann/ Corbis; p.174b ©Dave G. Houser/CORBIS; p.175a ©Bettmann/CORBIS; p.175b ©Arnold Newman/ Getty Images; p.177 ©O. Louis Mazzatenta/Getty Images; p.178 ©Glen Allison/Getty Images; p.181 ©O. Louis Mazzatena/Getty Images; p.184a ©Detlev van Ravenswaay/Photo Researchers, Inc.; p.184b ©Bettmann/CORBIS; p.187a ©Martin Harvey/ CORBIS; p.187b ©ZSSD/2003-2005 Minden Pictures; p.188a ©Don Bayley/iStockPhoto; p.188b ©rickt/Shutterstock; p.188c ©Shbukar Yalilfatar/ Shutterstock; p.193 ©Mark Savage/Corbis; p.196a ©iStockphoto; p.196b ©Dubi Preger; p.196c ©Lawrence Manning/CORBIS; p.197 ©Dubi Preger.

Additional photography by PhotoDisc/Getty Royalty Free; Eyewire/Getty Royalty Free; Corbis Royalty Free; Getty Images Royalty Free; Jacques Descloitres, MODIS Land Rapid Response Team/NASA/GSFC; Sam Dudgeon/Victoria Smith; Corel Royalty Free; Comstock Royalty Free; NASA photo, courtesy of the Lunar and Planetary Institute.